GIFTS OF UNKNOWN THINGS

GIFTS OF UNKNOWN THINGS

A True Story of Nature,
Healing, and Initiation from
Indonesia's "Dancing Island"

LYALL WATSON

Destiny Books
Rochester, Vermont

Destiny Books
One Park Street
Rochester, Vermont 05767
www.InnerTraditions.com

Destiny Books is a division of Inner Traditions International

Library of Congress Cataloging in Publication Data
Watson, Lyall.
  Gifts of unknown things : a true story of nature, healing, and initiation from Indonesia's "Dancing Island" / Lyall Watson.
      p. cm.
  Originally published : New York : Simon Schuster, c1976.
  Includes bibliographical references.
  ISBN 0-892681-353-9
  1. Occultism—Indonesia. 2. Parapsychology—Indonesia.
  3. Mental healing—Indonesia. 4. Ethnology—Indonesia. I. Title.
  BF1434.I5W37   1991
  001.9'09598–dc20   91-311167
                                                    CIP

Printed and bound in the United States

10 9 8 7 6 5 4

CONTENTS

There are more than thirteen thousand islands in the Indonesian Archipelago, scattered like stepping-stones between the continents of Asia and Australia; but you will not find Nus Tarian marked on any map.

Nevertheless, it exists.

Only I and the name have been changed.

LYALL WATSON
Lagoona, Bermuda

It was more like those myths, current in Polynesia,
of amazing strangers, who arrive at an island,
gods or demons,
bringing good or evil to the innocence of the inhabitants—
gifts of unknown things, words never heard before.

JOSEPH CONRAD in *Victory, 1915*

GIFTS OF
UNKNOWN
THINGS

FIRST STATE

FIRE

Eka Dasa Rudra, the greatest of Balinese sacrifices, is held only once every hundred years.

In 1963, the day fell on March 8, and as last preparations were being made in the mother temple of Besakih, high on the slopes of Gunung Agung, the dormant volcano began to rumble.

Then the "Navel of the World" exploded, sending a column of ash soaring fifty thousand feet into the air.

Wherever it fell, nothing was ever the same again.

STEP ONE

The Spirit Moves

We were three—two Javanese crewmen and I—in a tiny wooden prau.

She normally served the fishing rafts anchored in the shallow waters off Surabaja, but had been lured into the Banda Sea by my interest in the islands east of Bali, and by more rupiahs than the crew could normally earn in the course of an entire year.

I had had to resort to bribery because none of us had ever been into that part of the eastern archipelago, and, despite my eloquent appeals to their manhood, their national pride, and the souls of their seafaring ancestors, the other two were quite happy to leave things that way.

It was not a comfortable way to travel.

The little boat was just twenty feet long and shaped something like a Chinese junk. The deck sloped downwards to the bows, and in the center was a thatched hut where we cooked rice and fish and, when it rained, spread our rattan sleeping mats. The sails were patchwork oblongs of canvas and matting held together and aloft by a thicket of bamboo and string that I never had the courage to examine too closely. The steersman sat high on a box at the stern, using his bare feet to work an ironwood rudder hanging in a plaited sisal sling.

I needed a boat, but never even considered this unlikely craft until the day I saw her speeding close-hauled and bone-dry over a tidal race that left a visiting American yacht three times her size looking very wet and miserable.

And until I discovered that her name was Kembang Chili—the *Little Flower*.

Six weeks and many islands later, we lay becalmed and out of sight of land.

I enjoyed this brief respite from the tyranny of wind, but the crew kept looking up at the sky and saying nothing at all.

By midafternoon, streaks of high and icy cirrus had appeared overhead, all converging towards the east as though gathered in there by a giant hand.

It was the wrong month and too far north for cyclones, but in recent years the weather factories have shown scant respect for calendars, and sailors have learned that they can no longer afford to rely on seasons and predictions.

Nothing happened until sunset, when a long and unaccountable series of swells came rolling up out of the east.

Then we knew.

Revolving tropical storms are vast whirlwinds with a center of low pressure. Whether going under the local name of hurricane, cyclone or typhoon, they all go clockwise in the Southern Hemisphere and travel along at about ten knots. This speed may increase later as they swing around the pivot at the western limit of their track before recurving to the east, but most of the time they churn along a fairly straight and totally invisible line.

The best way to find out where you are in relation to the storm is to locate its center. Stand, if you still can, and face the wind. In this position south of the Equator, the vortex will lie at right angles to your left. If you raise your left arm until it is parallel to the ground, and reach back as far as you can without twisting the body, your index finger will be pointing provocatively at the calm and evil eye of the beast. If the wind remains steady, then it is coming directly towards you.

It did, and it was. We turned due north and ran.

This way the wind would always be behind us or, at the worst as the storm swept by, hitting us on the aft quarter or the beam.

It did all those things in the next ten hours as we lay flat on the decks.

I was glad the dark made it impossible to see what was going on. What I could feel was bad enough.

Sometime during the night the deckhouse blew away, carrying with it all our food and clothing, but the first hard gray light revealed that we were all there and, incredibly, so was

Little Flower—a little faded perhaps, but with every improbable petal of her hull and rigging still intact.

For a while the sea continued to stand over us with its fists clenched, but it was clearly running out of wind.

We had no idea where we were, but decided to set sail and swing south again, where we ought to run into one of a long chain of islands. And at sunset the following day, after another forty hours afloat, we did catch sight of land. A distant volcanic peak that rose up out of the waters like green and welcome Ararat.

By then it was too late to attempt a landing on an unknown shore, so we drifted under bare bamboo beyond the reefs and waited for the light.

The night was dark. We were in between moons, and the sky was still curtained by the cyclone's trailing skirts of cloud.

It was also very calm.

I could see a white line in the distance where the sea surged over the reef, but the water beneath us was black and a little hard to believe in. I lay on the deck and let my fingers fall until the warm and gentle grasp of surface tension restored it to liquid reality.

I let the mood take me, living only as it allowed, thinking only what it permitted me to think, but breathing deeply, very glad to be alive.

I have no idea how long that meditation lasted, but eventually something intruded sufficiently to attract my conscious attention.

Cassiopeia?

There was a pattern of light in the dark, one so reminiscent of the lazy shape of the Lady in the Chair that for a moment I thought the sky had cleared and I was seeing a reflection of the familiar constellation.

I even looked up, but it was black as ever overhead.

Then I realized that the lights were underwater, and somehow, this was a terrible shock.

Light belongs to the sun. Even before we knew it destroyed four million tons of matter a second in an endless thermonuclear blaze, it was obvious that our star was afire. A great fire, worthy of considerable reverence. The only local events that could touch it for power and majesty were forests in flame and volcanoes in the process of eruption. For most animals these were dangers to be avoided at all costs; but somewhere in the chain of circumstance and selection that set man apart from his ancestors stood an individual who stopped to take a closer look.

We know that Peking Man and at least one of the African ape-men kept a fire burning in their caves from time to time, but there is absolutely no evidence to show that either of them used this hearth for cooking. They may have valued it for the warmth it gave, or because it kept competitors and predators at bay; but I believe the truth is simpler and much more exciting.

Almost every culture has a myth that recounts the capture and domestication of fire. And in all these, fire was sought not because it might prove to be useful, but because it was fascinating. It still is. Despite all our sophistication, the minds of our children glow with the simple magic of matches; and even moribund adult imaginations are ignited for hours on end by the flickering expressions in a log fire. We are inflamed. As they were when they first captured the spirit of the sun and danced around it, or simply sat and watched this new and fascinating fetish come to life on the floors of their caves. There they tended it and fed it, keeping it alive and well: the earth's first divinity, enshrined on the altar of its hearth.

In the beginning it was an adventure. Not *just* an adventure, because it was probably our first. The first time any species in our system had made a major change in its way of life purely for the hell of it. Simply because it was fascinating, and because it seemed like a good idea at the time. Later we got down to the serious business of controlling fire, of exploring the night country and burning our way free of the shackles of gravity. And yet even today, when we build fires that blaze more fiercely than those in the sun itself, a single candle flame can still hold us in thrall.

It is because we attach so much significance to fire that we tend unconsciously to attribute all illumination to enlightenment. Lights in the night mean fires kindled and controlled by other men, by beings whose purposes are comparable and comprehensible to the human mind. So it comes as a shock to find them doing it where neither men nor flames belong—to see the lights burning deep underwater.

When I recovered from my initial disquiet, I realized there must be a biological explanation.

Many organisms make light.

At times the whole surface of the night sea glows with a sheet of cold fire that blazes wherever it is disturbed.

Schools of fish become rivers of flame, and dolphins burst

through the surface like rockets trailing showers of silver sparks.

Every moving vessel pushes ahead of it a billow of liquid phosphorus which is sometimes so bright that, standing on a tropical shore, I have been able to read the name illuminated on the bow.

All this glory can be attributed to tiny protozoans and crustaceans that harness chemical reactions, sparked by special enzymes, which produce a very efficient light with little heat.

To distinguish this kind of light from phosphorescence, which depends on previous illumination, biologists call it bioluminescence and know a little of its chemistry, but nothing of its purpose.

This is distressing, but the lights I saw in the deep that night disturbed me for quite another reason.

They had none of the flare and glitter one sees on the surface, producing instead a number of discrete cool pools of light like fluorescent tubes glowing in the gardens of a village in the valley.

As I watched, they grouped and regrouped, running through a whole zodiac of patterns, and then suddenly they all went out as though they were under some sort of central control.

Many deep-sea species of fish carry their own torches which act as lures and can be turned on or off at will. I have seen some that have lines of flares down the whole length of their bodies in patterns that differ from species to species, perhaps even giving each individual the chance to have his name up in lights. But nowhere have I come across any mention of the possibility of coordination, although I must admit it happens on land.

In Malaysia I have seen synchronous fireflies, perhaps ten thousand to a tree, all turning themselves on and off in perfect unison, transforming a line of mangroves on the bank of a moonless creek into a sparkling fairyland that creates itself anew with every pulsebeat. They seem to be all males, gathered together in one of the world's most extravagant mating displays. Each species has its allotted frequency, and the right sequence on an ordinary pocket flashlight in that part of the world can soon make you the center of an appropiate swarm of admiring female fireflies. And then what do you do?

I thought about this and tried to equate the firefly system with what I had seen down there deep beneath the *Little Flower*.

I felt certain there was a crucial difference.

There had been nothing mechanical or automatic about the pattern and position of the lights; and something very deliberate about the way they had all turned off together and without warning.

Perhaps *as* a warning?

Something could have frightened them, maybe even my casual dabbling at the surface.

I did not know, and I saw very little chance of ever resolving the mystery. I was busy mulling it over in my mind one last time before putting the whole experience away in a hoard

I keep against hard times—when all heaven broke loose.

The lights came on again all over the deep, and this time there were many more of them and much closer to the surface.

I did not move. I could not.

I simply lay and watched open-mouthed as the galaxy glowed there beneath me and came drifting slowly up, in perfect formation, towards the surface.

As they came closer, their resolution improved and I could see that each light was a sharp ovoid of cool blue glow with two lighter green flares within it near one end.

They came to a halt about ten feet below the boat and it was clear that each was itself about eighteen inches long.

All this time the *Flower* had been drifting in her usual quiet way, but then a larger swell flowed by and she leaned over on her side and grumbled a little about it.

Instantly the lights changed character.

Several went out altogether, a few turned from blue to green, and two very close to me flared up in a bright white burst of luminescence—and suddenly I knew who they were.

Squid!

The oceans abound in squid. They form the sole food of sperm and bottle-nosed whales and are eaten extensively by dolphins, seals, and oceanic birds. Huge concentrations of squid hovering just below the illuminated zone of surface waters may even be responsible for producing the phantom bottom reflections that haunt echo soundings of the deeper ocean basins.

We assume that squid occupy a wide variety of ecological niches in the sea, but most of our information about them is inferential, because they are so seldom seen. In the clear blue halls of a coral lagoon you may be lucky enough to find a chorus line of little ones swaying gently near the surface. On one wonderful occasion I saw a squadron jet right out of the water to man height and glide slowly back to the surface with their mantle flaps fully extended. Trawlers sometimes catch sick and slow-moving squid in their nets, but of the rest we know little except that some small ones leave the chitinous quills of their skeletons on the tidelines of our beaches, and some of the larger ones leave circular sucker scars the size of dinner plates on the skin of giant sperm whales.

In the thin skin of squid are small flexible bags of pigment connected to sets of radiating muscle fibers. Excited individuals blush in a variety of hues as these sacs change shape and send waves of color sweeping over their bodies. A dark squid floating over a light sandy bottom can blanch instantly and vanish without moving. It had not occurred to me before, but from what I could see that night from the deck of the *Little Flower*, it was obvious that the same sort of nervous control, and perhaps even the same pigments, were involved in displays after dark.

This was exciting enough, but there was more to come.

All the illuminated squid were now within three feet of the surface, forming a complete circle around the boat.

I counted sixty and then gave up. There must have been

several hundred. Every single one hovered with its short trailing group of tentacles gathered into a point that faced me like a nose between the bright green auras of its eyes.

I believe that the eye glow was a reflection produced by an almost metallic shield of tissue around the eye, because the main source of radiance clearly was within the leaf-shaped mantle sac which blazed with a strong still light.

At first I could see little difference between individual squid; some glowed brighter than others and a few seemed more green than blue, but this variation was cancelled out as the emphasis shifted from one part of the circle to another.

Then one of the crewmen stirred from his sleep and sat up and coughed.

In a flash the circle of squid grew several feet in diameter and, from this new and safer distance, began to throb with light like the display board on a giant computer.

And yet it was never that mechanical. From the moment the behavior began, I had absolutely no doubt it was purposive. As my Javanese companion stood up and walked round the deck to join me, the stress and frequency of the flashes followed him around the circle of agitated squid. It was not merely a luminous twittering of the sort one would expect from a flock of frightened starlings, but a controlled and excited exchange of emotion.

There is absolutely no way in which I can prove this assertion of intelligence, but I watched that group of animals very closely for a long time and there is no doubt in my mind that there was a conversation in progress—and that we were the subject under discussion.

We moved carefully up to the higher aft deck for a better view, and soon the entire squid community maneuvered itself into a glowing semicircle around us.

The illuminated conversation had now become desultory, confined to the occasional flash of casual comment, and I began to have the strange feeling that they were waiting for us to do something more interesting.

I tried waving my arms up and down and got a small neon response from the front row.

I would have loved to be able to respond in kind with a lamp or even a match. Several deep-sea sailors have told me of being bombarded by squid when they showed a light at night. But all our sources of illumination had been washed overboard in the storm.

I think a flashing torch might have evoked some fascinating reactions, but I am not sure it would have made a great deal of difference in the end.

The squid were indeed waiting, but not for us.

For a long time we simply watched each other.

At times it seemed their lights were suspended in air and we shared the same dark space. Then, gradually, the intensity of the squid luminescence began to fade.

When the change became apparent, I thought they were sinking back below the surface, but as I moved to look, they glowed again still in the same positions.

I grew a little impatient with the impasse and leaned over the side with the intention of splashing water at them, but my hand never touched the surface.

Directly below the boat I could see another light.

It was the same shape and color as those in front of me and seemed to be the same size until I realized, with a sinking sort of excitement, that it was still very deep down.

When I looked up to call my companion, I noticed that he

had been joined by the other crewman and that all the surface squid had disappeared.

The three of us and our *Little Flower* were alone with a light in the chasm below us that kept on growing relentlessly larger.

On October 11, 1492, the night before his first landfall in the New World, Columbus found the *Santa Maria* floating on a sheet of luminous water. The strange, even glow disturbed his sailors, who were long familiar with the sparkle of phosphorescence. This phenomenon is now well known in the Bahamas and is thought to be produced by organic matter brought to the surface by convection currents that cause upwelling of cold bottom water. But the glow is still so bright that astronauts have been able to pick it out from space as the last light visible to them from the earth.

Many seafarers have reported sights of huge glowing wheels, hundreds of feet in diameter, turning slowly just below the surface of the Indian Ocean. The most likely explanation for these is that they are produced by bioluminescent plankton being excited, and lighting up in series, as a wave form—perhaps from a distant submarine earthquake—passes by.

But even when these luminous marine phenomena have been more or less explained away, there remain some that cannot be classified quite so easily. These are the ones that have a more compact form and seem to move in a way that demonstrates some kind of volition.

Thor Heyerdahl tells of one night in the Pacific when three immense luminous bodies followed *Kon-Tiki* for several hours. He estimated their size to be greater than that of the raft, which was fifteen meters long.

By the time our body had completed its ascent to a point perhaps fifty feet from the surface, it was already clearly twice the size of our craft. We could see it on every side—a soft, clear glow billowing at the edges like a fluorescent cloud. The shape was roughly ovoid, similar to that of the squid, but through a depth of water it was impossible to pick out any details.

The *Little Flower* was drifting slowly along with a current moving parallel to the distant line of reef, and the aurora was keeping perfect pace with us below.

The crewmen were terrified. One kept running from side to side looking for a way out, and the other refused to look at all, sitting resolutely in the ruins of the deckhouse repeating the ritual "Peace be on you, and the mercy of Allah" over and over again.

I didn't know what to do.

I tried desperately to see some detail in the illumination, some concrete feature that would allow me to identify and classify it, to give a biologically meaningful account of it to my colleagues; but there was none.

I remembered my own exasperation with the incomplete reports of others in similar situations and understood for the first time the difficulty of being an eyewitness to anything really unusual. Objectivity is all very well, but it is possible only when you can describe your experience in terms of standard weights and measures. I did not know the frequency or the intensity of the light I was seeing, I could not provide an accurate record of its size, shape, or weight, and I had no scientific way of assessing its intelligence or intent. As a biologist in this situation, I was a total failure; but as a biological system, I continued to function very well. I can provide an account of my contact with the light that is totally subjective and of no practical value in any court of law or academy of science, but I believe it is nevertheless meaningful.

To begin with, I was both enthralled by the presence of the light and appalled by its size and my total lack of understanding. I do not remember feeling afraid; I was aware instead of a sense of privilege, the sort of synthesis of honor and awe that I usually associate with proximity to large whales. A feeling almost of exultation, of a kind of grateful elation that is very close to worship. A compound of "Praise be!" and "Why me?"

We lack the instruments necessary for recording stimuli of this order, and we seem to have lost the capacity for providing an appropriate response. It would help to be born again, but perhaps all we need to do is redevelop a kind of organic innocence, recapture the receptiveness of childhood and show a willingness to take part in and be filled, or emptied, by whatever it is that happens. I am beginning to believe that there may be no other way to experience, or even begin to explain, certain kinds of reality.

To make sense, you must have sensed. My sense of that light was overwhelming. I know it was alive and I believe it was conscious. During the time it was there beneath the boat, I felt a presence, the kind of certainty of life nearby that you have when you wake in a dark room and know beyond doubt that someone else is there with you. It was a presence that involved a certain amount of astonished recognition, like meeting for the first time in the flesh someone you already know well from film or photograph.

It did not last long.

As soon as I made that first fleeting contact, the light gathered itself together and shot off at tremendous speed back down into the deep and the dark.

We were alone again—and I felt like weeping.

It was a long night, and I spent most of it wondering what had happened. Until the moment the squid opened their illuminated conference, it had been only a field experience. A rare and magical episode of natural history of the kind that leaves you filled with wonder and delight. Then it had undergone a qualitative change and become significant in a totally different way. I couldn't put my finger on the moment that had first produced this shift in emphasis, until I remembered the light in the squid's eyes.

Squid are molluscs. Soft-bodied, unsegmented invertebrates belonging to a very old and diverse group of organisms. Most molluscs still have external shells and are restricted to fairly sedentary lives, attached to rocks or creeping along the ground, but despite this relative inactivity, some of them have excellent eyes. The common edible scallop lies on sandy undersea surfaces with the two halves of its corrugated shell held slightly apart to expose rows of vivid blue eyes, all focused and very much alert. In the tropics, there is a leaping conch that propels itself across exposed mud flats in foot-long bounds and will, if interrupted in this progress, extend a long fleshy tube and peer at you with an eloquent big brown eye. It is a very disconcerting experience to be scowled at by a snail. It is possible that the conch simply stares down all potential predators in this way, but it is very difficult on that ground alone to account for the presence of such an elaborate structure in a well-armored animal that does not need to be so sentient.

The development of this strange molluscan eye has gone even further in the highly mobile squid. All the oceanic squids have a complex eye with an iris, a variable-focus lens, and a retina with enough sensitive cells to make their color and pattern discrimination every bit as good as our own. Squid see as well as, if not better than, any other animals alive—or at least, their eyes have the capacity for doing so. This is uncanny, but what really worries me is what they do with so much information.

All molluscs have a nervous system consisting of just three small sets of knotted nerves, or ganglia. One lies around the mouth and seems to be involved only in feeding; another is positioned below the oesophagus and is responsible for the movement of fins, mantle, tentacles, and pigment cells; and a third rests on top of the gut. In the squid this third delicate tissue of nerve cells shows some differentiation, which suggests that it may be responsible for a variety of functions connected with complex behavior patterns that involve learning and association. It is in effect a brain, but a very simple and rudimentary brain. One too elementary to even begin to cope with the vast amount of information provided by the incredibly complex eye. It is a little like taking an expensive telephoto lens and sticking it on a shoe box.

The whole thing is absurd, but as a biologist I cannot just leave it at that. Nature does at times seem profligate and to produce some implausible schemes, but in the end they all tend to fit neatly together. There has to be a good reason for squid's eyes, but at that particular moment I could think of only one— and it still sounds so wildly improbable that I hesitate even to mention it. And yet, even now, it makes a mad kind of sense that is very persuasive.

Suppose, purely for the sake of argument, that the eye is exactly what it seems to be—a highly developed sense organ for the detection and collection of electromagnetic information in the range of frequencies occupied by visible light. And that the squid just happens to be attached to the back of this instrument to give it mobility.

Can you think of a better camera platform for oceanic

observation? Squid are sleek, speedy, and ubiquitous. There are billions of them, by day or night, on every level, at every temperature, in every part of the world ocean. Seeing without being seen.

Visitors are warned that this facility is under constant closed-circuit surveillance.

In all the nightmare world of parasitology, there are no more complex life histories than those of certain trematodes who are obliged to struggle through as many as eight trans-formations involving four different kinds of host. The common name "fluke" seems an apposite comment on the chances of any individual's completing an entire cycle without mishap.

One species, which aims to spend its adult life in the blood of domestic sheep, has, however, shortened the odds against itself by developing a technique that is interesting in the light of my feelings about squid.

Second-last stop for the fluke *Dicrocoelium dendriticum* is an ant. In the abdominal cavity of this insect host, it encysts yet again to produce a batch of tadpolelike larvae known as cercaria.

These are designed to make the final assault on a sheep, and they put themselves within striking distance of their goal by an extraordinary ploy. One of their number undergoes cellular changes, becomes very slim, and sneaks between the tissues of its host to attach itself to the major nerve ganglion around the oesophagus.

Once established there, this "brain worm" manages to

change the behavior of the ant so that it ignores all its normal colonial responsibilities and concentrates only on climbing to the top of the nearest grass stalk, where it anchors itself with its mandibles and waits.

Eventually, along comes a grazing sheep, and . . .

That kind of control is shattering. The ant is not producing a predictable reflex response to a simple stimulus. It is somehow being given a brand-new and highly complex set of instructions by the intruder riding on its brain.

I do not believe that squid are being manipulated in this way by a mind parasite, but it is a reminder that in our biological system, almost anything can happen. Complex relationships between entirely different organisms are quite common.

I have told several close friends of my experience with the squid, of my uncertainty about their eyes, and of my suspicion that they may have had something to do with the subsequent arrival of the mysterious luminary. Their responses range from credulous acceptance to incredulous hostility.

Both extremes are predictable, and neither is very helpful. Of the two, I find the instant believers more difficult to deal with because they are so totally committed to their particular brand of mysticism that they devour anything remotely resembling supportive evidence and assimilate it without question into the structure of their beliefs.

They may be right. I have great sympathy with many of their convictions. But I have equally great misgivings about any persuasion that hardens into dogma. And of all the fashionable creeds, none is more greedy, none more guilty of gobbling up ideas whole, than the cult of extraterrestrial intelligence.

I have absolutely no problem with the notion of life elsewhere. It is inconceivable that it should not exist and, existing, not grow into consciousness and intelligence. I think it probable that we will make contact with other beings, and possible that we may already have done so. It may even be true that there is continuous extraterrestrial involvement in our affairs. These are all fascinating notions and we would be foolish to ignore them. But as a terrestrial biologist (and therefore prone to be a bit dogmatic myself), I take exception to the growing tendency to attribute everything we cannot understand to alien intervention.

We have only just begun to scratch the surface of our own system. As a student, I worked with three ethologists who all did their doctoral theses on one aspect of the reproductive behavior of the three-spined stickleback. And they were only part of a community that dedicated twenty years of intensive effort to unraveling the complexities involved in the way of life of this one insignificant little freshwater fish. In the Amazon alone, there are another 2,500 species waiting to be worked on.

There are comparable situations in every science. As an archaeologist, I once worked in Jordan, where the Department of Antiquities lists over five thousand recognized sites. I found that only a handful were known at all well and that most of the rest had never even been given a surface survey.

We have hundreds of thousands of scientists busy exploring new frontiers, and almost as many involved in the painstaking process of retrieving old discoveries. We publish half a million scientific papers every year. But even if all these authors were to combine in a collective effort to work out the precise mechanism that enabled any of them to put just one word down on paper, it would probably take them a hundred years.

And with all this magic and mystery everywhere around us, why do we need to look for outside sources of excitement and explanation? That is very difficult for me to understand.

I am biased. I admit it. I have spent most of my life learning a little of the way of things here, following the weft in the pattern, trying to get to know the neighborhood. I like what I see. I enjoy the intricacy, and I feel party now to at least some of the intrigues. Damn it, I belong here and I will not see myself as some sort of heaven-sent stranger. I am an earthling and proud of our system and all its surprises. I acknowledge its weaknesses, I glory in its strengths, and I refuse to have any of them dismissed merely as gifts distributed amongst us by some patronizing interplanetary tourists.

We did not come into this world. We came out of it, like buds out of branches and butterflies out of cocoons. We are a natural product of this earth, and if we turn out to be intelligent beings, then it can only be because we are fruits of an intelligent earth, which is nourished in its turn by an intelligent system of energy.

Like most children of my generation, I was molded in an educational system that paid lip service to the notion of "team spirit," but continued to pit us against each other in situations that were purely competitive. I was taught to see myself as an entity, not only confined to the limits of my skin, but separated from others even by its color. Happily, that is changing. It had to change when we saw the first pictures of earth in its isolation, floating alone like an oasis in the desert of space. The concept of a "whole earth" has made it easier to accept that we are all in this together. We and the blue-eyed scallop and cattle and every creeping thing after his kind, but ultimately all of a kind. And the truly wonderful and devastating thing about this whole superb system is that there is something of the squid in each of us.

We are all the eyes and ears of the earth; and we think the world's thoughts.

There seem always to have been two ways of looking at the world. One is the everyday way in which objects and events, although they may be related causally and influence each other, are seen to be separate. And the other is a rather special way in which every thing is considered to be part of a much greater pattern.

From childhood, no matter what species we may belong to, we all learn to function in the first way because it has the highest survival value. It keeps the individual alive. The second way has little that is of such immediate and practical importance, and becomes a conscious concept only in certain systems, but it nevertheless plays a large part in every life.

There has never been any question of having to choose between the two. They merely represent the extremes of a spectrum of possible response. At one end is a scientist who sees everything in isolation, and at the other a mystic who experiences only a featureless flow. Both views are restricted and misleading, but there can be a meeting in the middle. When both physicists and mystics are asked for their description of how the world works, they give the same answers. It is almost impossible to distinguish between the two groups of quotations. All agree that there are two viable metaphysical systems, and that the truth lies in a reconciliation between them.

There is nothing new in this notion that all are parts of the whole and that the whole is embodied in all its parts. What is new is that our physical sciences are catching up with us and beginning to reinforce some very old and very basic biological perceptions.

Insight is beginning to substantiate intuition. In traditional physics, the world is thought to be made up of points. If you put a lens in front of an object, it will form an image of that object, and there will be a point-to-point correspondence between the two. This kind of relationship has encouraged us to assume that the whole of reality can be analyzed in terms of points, each with a separate existence. But certainty about this kind of concept has been shaken by quantum mechanics and by the development of a new system of recording reality without the use of lenses. By the invention of the hologram.

If you drop a pebble into a pond, it will produce a series of regular waves that travel outward in concentric circles. Drop two identical pebbles into the pond at different points and you will get two sets of similar waves that move towards each other. Where the waves meet, they will interfere. If the crest of one hits the crest of the other, they will work together and produce a reinforced wave of twice the normal height. If the crest of one coincides with the trough of the other, they will cancel each other out and produce an isolated patch of calm water. In fact, all possible combinations of the two occur, and the final result is a complex arrangement of ripples known as an interference pattern.

Light waves behave in exactly the same way. The purest kind of light available to us is that produced by a laser, which sends out a beam in which all the waves are of one frequency, like those made by an ideal pebble in a perfect pond. When two laser beams touch, they produce an interference pattern of light and dark ripples that can be recorded on a photographic plate. And if one of the beams, instead of coming directly from the laser, is reflected first off an object such as a human face, the resulting pattern will be very complex indeed, but it can still be recorded. The record will be a hologram of the face.

When the plate is developed and fixed, it will look like a totally meaningless jumble of very fine light and dark lines, but these can be unraveled. Simply take the plate into a dark room and illuminate it with the same laser. When you do this, you cancel out interference and what you get is the original pattern of light from the reflected source. Peering through the plate, you find yourself face to face. You get a very realistic view which is a great deal more than a two-dimensional portrait. Hologram means "whole record," so what you get is more than face value. You get all the information that light can provide about that face. The plate becomes a window. If you move your head to the side, you see the face in profile. Stand up and you get a view of the hairstyle.

This three-dimensionality is fascinating, but there is more. If you illuminate only a small part of the plate with a very narrow laser beam, you can still peer through this spot like a keyhole and see the whole face. No matter which part of the plate you choose to use, the view is still the same. This is the momentous thing about a hologram—every part contains the whole.

Any part of a hologram is a point in space, and yet it contains information about things at other points. Actually, the hologram plate is merely a convenient way of recording what is happening in that region of space. What happens is that there is a movement of light there, and it seems that embraced in that movement is a mass of information about events taking place in other spaces. Cameras have always told us that, but what the hologram says is that any old point in space will do. They all embrace everything happening everywhere.

David Bohm, an imaginative physicist based at Birkbeck College in London, has used this discovery as the starting point for a new description of reality which he calls the enfolded order.

Newton's laws of motion make it possible to determine the position occupied by an object in space at a series of times. They assume that it is the same object which moves from place to place. Bohm suggests that what happens is that the object does not move, but is created again in each new position. It folds like the tents of the Arabs and silently steals away; and each time it unfolds and reappears, its form is generally similar, but there are differences in detail. In other words, our description of an object, what we like to think of as objective reality, is merely an appearance which is abstracted from a hidden flow. No unfolded object has an independent, substantial existence in its own right; it depends on the folded order for its form.

Imagine an insoluble ink droplet placed in a viscous fluid. If the fluid is stirred slowly by a mechanical device, the droplet will be drawn out into a fine thread folded into the system in such a way that it is no longer visible to the naked eye. But if the machine is reversed, the fine thread will slowly gather together until it once again unfolds and appears as a visible droplet.

Suppose that a droplet is folded into the syrup in this way. Another droplet is then introduced at a slightly different position, and it too is folded in the same number of times. Repeat this with a whole series of droplets in progressively different positions. Then start unfolding.

What will happen is that each of the droplets will appear briefly before being folded back in again in the opposite direction. And if the stirrer moves fast enough to produce, say, twenty-four droplets per second like the frames in a film, an object that looks like a single droplet will appear to move through the fluid. There is, however, no such object. It is an illusion whose existence depends entirely on the fluid.

With the hologram we have found a way of showing how this works for light, but the same rules could apply to sound or to the movement of electrons.

So what Bohm is suggesting is that matter, all matter, can be understood as a set of forms, which enjoy a certain amount of autonomy, but are really based on a process—a sort of universal flux. Matter is independent enough to be investigated in itself, but only up to a point. You can discover a particle's position or its velocity, but not both. Some things can never be known, because ultimately there are no particles.

So I and the squid, the sea and the reef, and the rocks on which we all rest, are only relatively stable forms derived from the flux. Anything that can be seen or heard or handled by scientific instruments is an abstraction unfolded from the invisible, inaudible, intangible ground of all matter.

I like the idea. It fits in rather well with our general experience of things. In fact, it even begins to make some kind of sense of purely mental forms. Thoughts can be considered as particular objects unfolded from the deeper ground movement of mind. And everything, the whole of existence, can be seen to have its origins in a single source—universal life energy.

Exercising my bias as a biologist, I suspect that there must be degrees of foldedness. I would expect to find that living organisms have some sort of hot line, a more direct connection with the energy source than inanimate matter could have or would need. And that we lose this link, our lifeline, we cease to be subscribers to the service, when we die.

I have seen some extraordinary holograms in which a lens has been included as part of the scene. As in ordinary photographs, whatever lies behind the lens is distorted, but as you move towards or away from the hologram plate, the objects seen through the lens are magnified or diminished appropriately.

Theoretically, one could produce holograms including microscopes and telescopes that would give you a view of everything from single cells to double stars. Then you could carry one small chip around as a charm, a sort of concentrated cosmos imprisoned in a signet ring. But all that effort would be pointless, because in essence that is what we already have, in every cell of our bodies. That is what the lifeline means. It is the lens in the hologram, our connection to the cosmos. Direct dialing to anywhere in the universe.

This notion of continuity keeps cropping up.

It can be found in the works of Whitehead and Leibniz, of Spinoza and Heraclitus. It is embodied in the poetry of Whitman and Blake, of Verlaine and Baudelaire. It is a recurring theme in all Hindu Upanishads and in the Egyptian Book of the Dead. It is the mainstay of every ancient mystical tradition and it is the essence of the modern science of ecology (although few who use the word seem willing or able to take it to its logical limits). But most important of all, a sense of oneness is at the core of every system of belief, every view of the world, held by every child everywhere.

Children have a very powerful sense of the propriety of certain things. They believe that rocks and houses are alive, that bears and elephants have feelings, and that it all matters. Every child of five knows everything there is to know; but when children turn six we send them to school, and then the rot sets in.

I wish there were some way of reconciling formal education and natural knowing. Our inability to do this is a terrible waste of one of our most valuable resources. There is a fund of knowledge, a different kind of information, common to all people everywhere. It is embodied in folklore and superstition, in mythology and old wives' tales. It has been allowed to persist simply because it is seldom taken seriously and has never been seen to be a threat to organized science or religion. It *is* a threat, because inherent in the natural way of knowing is a sense of rightness that in this time of transition and indecision could serve us very well.

Both poet and scientist deal in human truths, but we have relinquished control of our destiny to science alone—and that is a mistake, because scientists are missing something. Galileo thought comets were an optical illusion. We know they are not, but our scientists have delusions of their own. There are whole areas of experience left virtually unexplored because they conflict with current orthodoxy. Most of us pass by on the other side with our senses discreetly averted, but fortunately there are some whose curiosity cannot be so simply circumscribed. Poets and children and other wise and primitive people often stop to look and wonder. Some try to tell of it, but the words they use are simple ones, full of mystery and rhyme, and the scientific journal has yet to be founded that would accept a report in blank verse whose sense was in the sound and not in the syntax.

The grammar and the goals of science are incompatible with certain kinds of truth. There are levels of reality far too mysterious for totally objective common sense. There are things that cannot be known by exercise only of the scientific method.

How then can we affirm the existence of that which is folded? How can we validate experience which does not readily lend itself to description in the precise language of technology?

I think there is at least one way—the one I found in Indonesia.

I learned to dance.

When dawn dispersed the night of the lights, we could see where we were.

The *Little Flower* lay waiting just outside a reef, and beyond that was a lagoon backed by a breathtaking landscape.

To our right, at the south end of the island, stood an old volcanic cone. It was perhaps a thousand feet high, still perfectly conical, but weathered and wrinkled with forest, fringed with a tracery of palm.

The northern slope ran away into a ripple of hills that rose and fell in an easy rhythm across to our left where the island ended in another peak, less than half the size of the first, with its crater breached by a jagged line of lava.

As the sun began to rise behind the island, a scattering of tall, branching lontar palms came into silhouette along the skyline, and outcrops of old and rusty ash singled out the first warm tints of the day.

The lagoon was glassy, and suspended beneath the island hung its mirror image, separated from it by nothing more than a thin white strip of sand.

The whole scene, so clear and composed with its theatrical

backlighting, was totally unreal, like an elegant diorama in a natural history museum.

With all sail set, we moved slowly along the curved line of the reef, looking for a channel. There were several small flat islets of raised coral, fretted into razor-sharp edges and covered with a thorny shrub. At one point stood a tiny volcano, a daughter cone or perhaps even a third-generation descendant of the peak in the distance.

It wasn't until we came close to the northern end of the island itself that we found a way through the outer defenses and into the lagoon. A hundred yards from the shore stood two volcanic pillars, and between these sentinels was a natural passage of deep water. We went through and on into the shallows with a long white beach curving away on our left, broken here and there by patches of mangrove.

Then we rounded a point of the island, and tucked away at the end of the beach at the foot of the smaller peak stood a village. As we got closer, we could see that it was quite large, with about fifty or sixty thatched houses clustered around the bright white metal on the minaret of the mosque. My companions breathed a thankful "Allah is great," knowing they had at least something in common with the people in this unknown place.

Most Javanese are Muslim, but the eastern islands are largely Christian, with a sprinkling of unrepentant headhunters in places like Asmat. We had no idea what to expect here.

What we got was a tumultuous welcome.

One moment the beach was deserted except for a skinny black dog scavenging along a line of outriggers that leaned drunkenly on the sand. The next it was swarming with children, leaping up and down and shouting greetings and instructions. As our sails were furled, several of the older ones swam out and clambered on board, but when they saw me, all of them dived straight back in.

I tried greeting them in Indonesian and they screamed with laughter. One of them swallowed so much water that we had to haul him out and give him artificial respiration. The others soon regained their courage, and by the time we had anchored and were starting to wade ashore, all three of us had a clump of kids attached to each arm.

At the water's edge was a group of men and women, waiting much more quietly. They formed a semicircle, and a tall man in a faded *kebadja* jacket stepped forward. He said his name was Hashim and that he was the *kepala desa*, the village head. He spoke the ritual greetings, we replied in kind, and then he turned and led the way up the beach.

In the shade of the first coconut palms on the edge of the village stood a line of young girls wrapped in identically patterned kains and wearing white cotton shirts. One offered us betel nut from a carved wooden box, another brought leaves of the siri vine, and a third a tray of fine white lime. Availing ourselves of their hospitality, we took a little of each and started chewing.

If you keep salivating long enough, the entire chemistry of the mixture alters and turns your mouth bright red. This makes everyone else very happy and the chewer slightly high. After two days without food or drink, I found that it made me feel like flying.

Then the dance began.

It started suddenly, with a chord I shall never forget. It was played by two drummers who sat cross-legged on the ground and by three men who launched a concerted attack on a battery of twelve brass gongs of descending sizes suspended from a rack between two palms. There was an appalling precision about the sound that by-passed the ears altogether and struck straight at the soul. It hit a resonant frequency that left all around me—the people, the palms, and even the dog on the beach—vibrating in sympathy. Then the percussive assault continued with a cascade of sound that swept everything along before it.

Three of the girls in traditional costume moved with it out onto the edge of the sand and began to hover there in the sun. Like mayflies suspended over a bright summer stream, they skimmed over the surface, dipping and rising, spinning and turning, sweeping with arms outstretched to touch the music in the air. Faster and faster, moving together and apart, they began to weave exquisite patterns, building a web of light and movement that rose and rose, until it fell. Two of the girls went with it and remained kneeling there, eyes cast down and hands folded in their laps. The third kept on dancing. She was very young, eleven or twelve perhaps, with her slender insect body wrapped in a cloth cocoon.

She started slowly, with an easy grace and rhythm, doing very little more than move her hands in a delicate counterpoint to the music, but at the same time she was somehow shifting the balance of her body in a way that introduced an entirely new tempo. I never saw the movement. I only know she managed to flow effortlessly and invisibly through a series of positions so eloquent that she telescoped time, and I understood every word.

She told of myths and heros from a land in the west; of stars and ships and voyages and places fit to rest.

She conjured up the heat of the sun and the strength of the monsoon.

She remembered the times of hunger and drought, and the seasons of plenty and song.

She sung of wars of conquest, and battles of restitution; of love and birth, and rice and wine: of death and destitution.

She danced us both a welcome and a history of her people.

She was Tia.

And this was Nus Tarian, the Dancing Island.

STEP TWO

Separate Waters

First light.

The muezzin stands.

He calls to the east, "*Allahu akbar.*"

Turning to the south, "Allah is great."

Arms out to the west, "Allah is great."

And to the north, "Allah is great," again.

A cock crows somewhere in the village, diffidently.

"There is no god but Allah."

Another, and then a third, reply in kind with growing confidence in the dawn.

"And Muhammad is His messenger."

Smoke rises gently in still air over thatch as palm frond and driftwood are blown back to glowing life in each hearth.

"Come to prayer."

"Prayer is better than sleep."

The pulley on the well squeaks rhythmically as women drift into the sandy square beside the mosque to draw water in the old wooden bucket.

"Come to contentment."

Buffalo in their corral on the beach stand and shake their

scimitared heads. Soon it will be time to return to the *padi* fields.

"Allah is great."

"There is no god but Allah."

The muezzin comes down the ladder from the minaret, stepping carefully over the missing rung. He straightens his black *songkok* cap and steps out onto the terrace of the mosque, where he waits to join the men in morning prayer.

Each day the dance began again in the village of Kota Rendah.

I watched it from my new home near the school on the hill.

To repay the boundless hospitality of the people, I taught English, and as my Indonesian improved, I was able to tackle mathematics and then geography and biology.

There had been no regular guru on Nus Tarian for several years, and so Pak (all older men are called "father") Hashim suggested I move into the house set aside for a teacher.

It was a tiny two-room hut with walls of leaf mat and woven cane. The roof was thatched with palm leaves split down the midrib and laid like shingles so that the long leaflets hung down in a whispering fringe. The floor was slatted driftwood raised three feet from the ground to keep it cool and free of sand. Windows were holes cut into the walls, but my front door was a magnificent old carving, fretted and fitted with louvered shutters opening onto a small veranda. Hanging from the open rafters were ferns roughly potted in coconut husks and pink-and-white wild orchids growing in bamboo tubes.

Most days I wandered down to the beach while the deep vocal drone from the mosque still rolled on out of the village like a river of sound that lost itself on the sand.

On the morning it all began, the tide was out.

Ghost crabs burst pale green and rectangular out of burrows in the sand and, bodies raised high on absolute tiptoe, skittered around on their points from one piece of jetsam to the next.

Their eyes are on stalks and hinged so that they can be laid back into protective sockets in the carapace while the crabs are burrowing, or raised like signal flags when they are foraging. Evolving on unprotected shores where they had to rush down to feed between one huge wave and the next, they can outrun and outmaneuver most terrestrial predators. The only way to get a close look at them is to sit absolutely still and to flick small objects out onto the sand in a way that attracts their attention and brings the closest ones in *en bourrée* to investigate.

I was playing this game with the crabs when I saw Tia, the tiny dancer, shaking a sleeping mat out the door of the house of her uncle. She waved and, a little later, came down to the beach to join me. It was dawn, and light was bright and clear on the peak of Gunung Api, the "fire mountain" at the far end of the island.

We walked together down the beach, and a small and mottled heron flew up at our feet, landed ahead on the sand, ruffled, walked, watched us coming on, lengthened its neck in new alarm, and flew another few reluctant yards.

Every time it took flight it uttered a sharp, broken "kew" sound on a descending tone.

"*Puchong laut,*" said Tia, and laughed gently. "He sings a green song."

For a moment I simply enjoyed the bird and the poetry of her description, but then it occurred to me that only I knew it as a little green heron. In fact it isn't very green at all. The literal translation of her name for it was something like "longlegs of the sea."

"Why green?" I asked her.

"That is his color. His voice is like a sharp new leaf or a thorn."

"Not brown?"

"No, of course not. Brown is the sound of *katak.*"

Katak was the local toad. The common lumpy one that propped itself up near lights in the village at night and produced a derisory sound that was indeed rather brown.

The idea was beginning to grow on me.

"What makes a black sound?"

"Buffalo. And thunder."

"White?"

"The sea where it touches the sand."

Now I was really hooked.

Tia was giving me these examples without hesitation, as though she were used to hearing sounds in color. And what really appealed to me was that the colors were totally appropriate. They were the colors of the objects producing the sound.

I thought of the tawny roar of a lion; of the scarlet scream of a macaw; of the deep bronze boom of an important bell, and of how the little ones that tinkled tended to be silver.

" 'Tia,' " I said her name clearly. "What color is that?"

"Pink when *you* say it, like an orchid. Paman Abu makes it yellow."

"And 'Abu'?"

"Sometimes blue, sometimes brown. It depends."

"On what?"

"The one who says it, and if the person feels friendly."

She was clearly getting a little impatient with all this talk about something so obvious, but I couldn't leave it alone.

"All sounds have colors?"

"*Astaga!* You did not know?"

"No."

"How can you listen to talk or music without color?" Her eyes were full of pity. "When the drums talk, they lay a carpet of brown, like soft sand on the ground. A dancer stands on this. Then the gongs call in green and yellow, building forests through which we move and turn. And if we lose our way, there is always the white thread of the flute or the song to guide us home."

She shook her head in sorrow and dismay, and faced with the wisdom of this twelve-year-old, I felt like a backward child.

Later I had the chance to test her with a variety of sounds. I chose more than a hundred, and when I questioned her about them again after several months, she still gave me exactly the same responses. Tia had multicolored hearing. She lived permanently in a roseate world with a unity of sight and sound that the rest of us, sensory cripples, can experience only fleetingly with the help of hallucinogenic chemicals.

And yet that word "hallucination" worries me. It is a much too convenient label we attach to anything that doesn't happen to fit our current description of reality. I suspect that most, if not all, children customarily link several senses together. Physiologists call it sensory blending or synesthesia and usually deal with it only when discussing the obvious linkage between taste and smell. But it seems likely that all our senses are ultimately interconnected and that every one of us depends, for fine discrimination of delicate emotional shades, on a blend of information.

Tia knew her own people better than I, but she astonished me with her ability to make rapid, sensitive, and invariably correct judgments about situations based on her appreciation of tone and color. When I or someone else was about to get angry, she would know instantly by what she called *warna sakit*, "sick colors," in our voices.

One day in school, I talked about this and most of the children seemed to think it was self-evident. They were not all as adept as Tia, but there was general agreement about which colors went with particular sounds. We compiled a list of colored words and, looking for some pattern in them, found that each of the usual vowel sounds in Indonesian had its characteristic color.

Barat, "the west," was a red word, so the vowel "a" was usually red. The "e" sound is almost totally suppressed in Indonesian, so we decided that it had to be gray. The nearest you get to hearing it is in *belum*, which sounds more like "bloom"; it is one of those marvelous flexible words and means everything from "not quite yet" to "never." The people hate to give an outright negative answer to anything, so even if you ask an octogenarian spinster if she is married, the answer you will get is *"belum*—not yet."

A very polite and suitably gray word.

The sound of the vowel "i" is sharp, as in English "gin," and it is white. It is the color of *iklim*, "the climate," and every maiden aunt, or *bibi*. "O" is round, as in "order," and so a shop, or *toko*, is black. The vowel "u" is pronounced "oo" as in *buku*, "a book," and everyone agreed that books were blue.

There was a close relationship between pitch and brightness. Deep voices, big drums, and low-pitched sounds all had dark colors—blues, browns, and black. High-pitched sounds were always attached to brighter colors. The strident call of the sulfur-crested cockatoo was white, like the bird. A loud whistle was accompanied by a blinding flash, and one little boy even claimed to be able to locate mosquitoes in the dark by seeing the fine white light of their whine.

This started me thinking for the first time that the colors need not be mental associates of the sound, but could exist as sensory inputs in their own right. It may well be true that the world actually is as these children, and probably all others everywhere, see it. When the rest of us grow up, we stop doing things that way. We no longer feel the texture of a sound or see the image of a taste. We miss the smell of the sunset and the color of a peacock's call. We put away sensory blending along with other childish things. It seems a pity.

Eventually the little green heron grew tired of retreat and, sitting hunched up on a fallen tree trying to look resentful and invisible all at the same time, let us walk on by.

I was still excited by my discovery of Tia's ability to hear colors, but didn't want to push too hard, so we changed the subject. Or at least, I thought we had.

"You haven't been in school this week."

"I keep house for Paman Abu. My cousin Ali has only eight years and needs help."

Abu kept the village store, and I knew he had taken his prau to guide the *Little Flower* to another island several days distant where the crewmen could get supplies. They were anxious to return to Java, and I had paid them off with a letter of credit to my bank.

"When will he return?"

"By sunset today." She was very certain.

"How do you know?"

"I have seen him coming."

We had reached the point that conceals the village from the sea, and now the whole horizon lay open to the north and west beyond Pintu, the gateway between the two sentinel rocks on the reef.

"I see nothing."

"He comes. And with another ship."

I looked in the direction she indicated, but I could still see nothing. And my eyes are very good.

"Show me."

"*Wah!* Who then is the guru that I must even teach you how to see?"

"Never mind all that. Just show me those ships."

"One cannot see the ships!"

"But you said—"

"I said Paman Abu was near, and he was not alone. I see no ships, merely the signs of their coming."

Now I was thoroughly confused.

I began to think that Tia must be either precognitive or in telepathic contact with her uncle.

Neither of these possibilities would have surprised or disturbed me, and I would have been quite content with her prediction if she had made it with her eyes closed.

That kind of "seeing" I have grown accustomed to in my friendship with western psychics, but I could not understand why Tia was looking so intently out over the ocean.

There was nothing out there that I could see.

"Look, Tuan." Now she was being very patient and polite with me. "What happens when two fighting cocks dance?"

I shrugged.

"You have seen them in the village. They fly near to each other, then stop." She held up her hands about six inches apart. "It is as though they run into a wall and can go no farther. Each strains to attack, but neither can because something holds them back."

Now the child was teaching me ethology. But I listened.

"Well, you can see this wall if you look carefully. It is a dark line, like smoke. And it hangs there between them until something pushes it away. Then the cocks hit each other with their feet. And the one over which the smoke passes will always lose. We all know this."

I didn't. I felt naked and did not know what to say, but she wasn't expecting a response.

"Dogs and buffalo do the same. And people. Whenever you grow angry in the school, your smoke covers the whole class, but it passes quickly because we let it go. The same is true of any strong feelings. Fear and love and hate all make shadows, but their colors are different. And all blow away as smoke will in the wind unless they touch another of their color and meet to form a wall."

"And Abu's prau produces such a color?" I thought I could see where she was leading, but Tia shook her head.

"If you simply walk on the beach as we are doing, you have no special color. But if you travel with a purpose, it is different. When you go somewhere important or you return home from a long journey, you build a shape around you and it reaches out ahead to touch your destination. Last night, looking at the sea, I saw the shape and color of my uncle and I knew already then that he was coming. This morning I see it more clearly, and with it something else I do not know. It can only be new people."

With that she turned and left me, going back to her chores.

I stood there on the beach for a long time staring at the horizon. I squinted at it, I looked at it quickly out of the corner of my eye, I tried to imagine shapes and forms reflected in the clouds. I looked for waves and smoke and envelopes of energy.

I saw nothing.

But at noon the children were calling out that two boats could be seen, and just before sunset Abu came drifting into the lagoon in his little prau followed by the larger lateen sail of a Bugis trader.

In 1780 a Monsieur Bottineau, an obscure civil servant on Île de France (now Mauritius), wrote to his Minister of Marine and announced that he had discovered a way of detecting ships while they were still below the horizon.

The Governor tested him by recording his predictions in a special register for four years. He was able to anticipate the sighting of vessels coming from Europe so often, and sometimes as much as three days in advance of their arrival, that he won a great deal of money in wagers.

Bottineau used his winnings to return to Europe himself in

an attempt to interest people there in his new science, which he called *nauscopie*. At first he had no success, but after the French Revolution Bottineau seems to have got close enough to the new seat of power to persuade Jean Paul Marat to write to scientists in England on his behalf. Nothing came of it, and the marine visionary died in misery in 1802 in Pondicherry.

We know little of Bottineau's natural radar system except that he used only his naked eye and seems to have trained himself to see some very faint indication, like an extremely attenuated cloud somewhere near the horizon, which heralded the arrival of a sailing ship. He apparently believed that the movement of the vessel produced an envelope of vapor around her which grew steadily and began to project itself ahead of the ship, remaining invisible until it interacted in some way with similar vapors produced by another ship or a mass of land.

Making allowances for their differences in background, Bottineau's concept is remarkably like that of Tia. Both felt that there were vaguely visible energetic patterns projected over the horizon. Both acknowledged that it was a two-way system, depending on an interaction between transmitter and receiver. But I suspect Tia was closer to the truth in her assumption that it was the people on the boat and not the boat itself that mattered.

Every cell in a body and every molecule and atom in that cell is in a state of constant vibration. These minor local disturbances add up together to produce enough energy to change the electrical and magnetic properties of the space they occupy. And news of this change travels at the speed of light to other spaces.

Because our constitutions are all different, each of us resonates on a particular frequency that is as individual as a fingerprint. But as humans, we are sufficiently alike to ensure that our unique transmissions all fall within a certain wave band and can be received by others of our kind.

All biological systems are in constant communication with each other and with the outside world in this way.

We are all radar units. Our bodies emit quite large amounts of energy in the same high frequencies used by most radar transmitters. We radiate microwaves about a thumbnail wide. Patterns of these waves explore everything in the vicinity, so all the time we are with other people we are unconsciously probing them and being touched in turn by their transmissions.

If sensitive radiometers are set up around a living body to detect its emission, they show that radiation varies as physiological changes take place. A sick person produces a less powerful transmission than a healthy one; and a normal body sends out extra flares of radiation whenever it displays any strong emotion. Even with the relatively insensitive equipment now being used, it is possible to detect these outbursts from thirty or forty feet.

Our electronic range is limited by the fact that the human body is a comparatively weak source of power. Our nervous system, however, has many of the same semiconducting properties as a transistor and can magnify weak electrical effects as much as a million times. This makes us very sensitive receivers, quite capable of picking up signals from a distance. Theoretically, there is no reason why we should not be able to detect messages coming from similar organisms many miles away, possibly from points beyond our visual horizon and perhaps even from transmitters on the other side of the planet.

Some people can hear radar microwaves. If their ship or plane is swept by a radar beam, they pick it up as a buzzing sound, like a swarm of passing bees. If we all share something of this sensitivity, it would account for that uneasy feeling we sometimes have of being watched—and then turning round suddenly to find that it is true.

At the University of Delaware, rhesus monkeys were stared at by a human they could not see. He simply peered at them through a hatch at random intervals, but every time he did so, there were distinct changes in the patterns of their brain waves and they began to behave as if suddenly depressed. In a comparable study with humans, it was found that a person who is looked at a lot tends to have a higher heart rate than someone who isn't.

It is possible that many of those we label paranoid may simply be individuals with a greater than normal sensitivity to the microwaves that accompany this kind of directed attention.

The wavelength of visible light is much shorter than microwaves. Our eyes are just not designed to see long waves, and even those exceptional people who can push their visual limits into the infrared region of the spectrum are still responding to radiation one thousandth the length of the shortest radar waves.

So it is unlikely that people like Tia can see microwaves themselves, but their special combination of sight and hearing could make them sensitive to some kind of visual effect. The blending of the two senses probably reduces the threshold of each in a way that opens up areas not normally available to either sense operating independently.

There are sporadic reports from all over the world of

people who claim to be able to hear the soft music of the aurora borealis or the hum of a passing meteor. Perhaps Bottineau was one of these and any of them could, with sensitivity training, be able to detect the approach of other people at a distance. The surface of a calm sea, with a long ocean horizon and no conflicting radiations, could be perfect conditions for pushing this sensitivity to unusual limits.

There are clearly several physical mechanisms to which this kind of sensitivity can be attributed. Electronics and systems engineering are taking their place alongside playing cards and dice in parapsychological investigation as researchers become aware of field effects associated with living systems.

This is a development which is bound to produce scientific interest in hitherto unrecognized biological aptitudes, but it is important to remember that these talents are by no means new. They remain unrecognized only by a technology that requires very rigid mechanical demonstrations of reality; and they can be explored by that discipline only so far as they continue to abide by its rules and restrictions. Others, less tied to such intellectual restraints, have known about and used these talents for a very long time.

His ultrasensitivity in a conservative early industrial community made Bottineau a curiosity, a freak who was led into a desperate attempt to capitalize on his ability, but succeeded only in dying in poverty and rejection.

For Tia, a similar talent was nothing special. She saw it as just another small and satisfying way of doing things. And the island community let her do it easily and comfortably, accepting the information she provided as naturally as we take that given to us by radio and television.

Both she and Bottineau were deviants, but the ways in which their respective communities dealt with them and with their talents provide some measure of relative social maturity.

In fairness, though, I must admit that Tia was not the only strange person on Nus Tarian and that even these tolerant island people were eventually driven to a point of opposition and denial.

Ibu Suri was incredibly old, dark and craggy-faced, with a mouth stained red from the everlasting chewing of betel.

Her long silver-gray hair still hung down to her waist, and she groomed it often with a pink plastic brush, sitting on the stairs of her isolated home down on the shore of the lagoon.

She had no children of her own, but she rated the courtesy title of Ibu, "mother," because there were always young people in the clearing beside the house, waiting to do whatever she asked.

She asked little but demanded a great deal, because she had something invaluable to give.

Every afternoon except Friday she would appear on her veranda and stand there for a moment, easily balanced on her feet, back straight and her eyes shining. She would take a long look round at all those waiting in the shade and then glide down the stairs and across the sand, well over eighty years old and yet still moving like a dancer.

For she *was* a dancer, the best the island had ever known.

Now, step by step, gesture by gesture, through all the old and intricate forms, she taught the things she knew.

It was wonderful to watch.

Ibu Suri would take a young girl from the group and stand behind her with the child's body tucked into her own, forcing it to follow every nuance of her form.

With the small head under her chin, she worked the limbs like a puppet's, wrapping her arms around the girl's, manipulating the hands and positioning each finger in turn.

It was instruction by body instead of by book.

The pupil wore the teacher's skin, fitting herself precisely to the mold of her mentor. The old teacher's legs became her legs, perfectly in tune, shuffling, pushing and kicking her feet into the right positions at the proper time.

And with Ibu Suri talking all the time.

"*Hai!* So, like this. Yes. Now back, higher, higher . . . there! And down again. Round and down. Eyes to the left. *Kiri!* Left. This is of the past, the left is past. Then slowly back to the front, back to the present. *Wah!* Pick up your foot. *Bagus,* that's good. Gently now, listen to the drum . . . *kupak, kupak, kupak-upak-upak, a-peng.*"

The old lady carried a whole percussion section on her tongue, and she would drum and gong her way around the clearing, shaping the girl's body and making it remember.

"Let's go! One, two and one, two. Up, down . . . easy, now. *Kupak, kupak; kupak-upak-upak; kupak, kupak; o-pikapika-pik; a-trrrrrrrih, a-peng!*"

This would go on for hours, Ibu Suri stopping only briefly while she wiped her sweat away with an old and tattered kain.

Then, finally, she would shout, "*Tjelaka!*" and collapse in the shade of the old *sukun,* a dark green breadfruit tree that grew beside the house.

All this time the other children watched intently, nobody moving until it was all over. Then one of the girls would go indoors to fetch her a drink of cool water scented with a little nutmeg, while everybody else moved in closer to listen to Ibu Suri talk.

One afternoon I joined the circle and, as Ibu Suri massaged her legs to keep them supple, she told one of the old stories:

"The first people lived in a land to the west. The world was the same in those times as it is today; it has always been the same. There were nine families of mankind, just as there are nine clans now in our village. Amongst the clan of kerbau, the buffalo, was a man named Ameta, which in the old language means 'dark as night.' He was neither married, nor had he any children. He went off hunting one day and chased a deer into a pond, where it drowned. When he pulled the body out, he found a coconut impaled on its antler, though at that time there were no coco palms anywhere in the world.

"Returning to his hut, Ameta planted the nut in the earth, and next morning a palm began to grow. In three days it was tall and bearing blossoms. He climbed the tree to collect palm juice, but slashed his finger, and blood fell onto a leaf, where it mingled with the sap from the stem. When he returned three days later, the leaf had changed into a little girl. He wrapped her carefully in a cloth, took her home and named her Hainuwele, which means 'frond of the coco palm.'

"Hainuwele grew quickly, and in three more days she was tall and beautiful. But she was lonely and restless, too. Fortunately, at about that time there was to be a great Maro dance in the place of the Nine Dance Grounds. Then, as always when the people start to dance the Maro, the women sit in the center and pass betel nut to the men, who stamp out a large ninefold spiral around them.

"Hainuwele was chosen to be amongst those in the middle on the first night of this festival. On the second night, on the second dance ground, she was chosen again; but this time instead of passing out betel, she gave each dancer a gift of a beautiful porcelain dish. And on each new ground, her gifts became more and more precious. On the third, it was copper boxes; on the fourth, gold earrings; and on the fifth, glorious bronze gongs. By the time the festival reached the ninth and last night, the other dancers were so jealous of Hainuwele that they conspired together and trampled her to death beneath their whirling feet.

"When Hainuwele failed to return home at dawn the next day, her father cast an oracle of coco palm leaves, discovered the death, recovered her body, and cut it into many pieces, which he buried again all over the island. By the time of the next full moon, each and every portion had turned into an unknown thing that up to that time had never existed anywhere else on earth. One of these gifts was a crop of rice, so that ever since then, all dancers have been reminded of their crime three times every day.

"But," Ibu Suri ended, staring sadly down at her own brown and dusty feet, "it seems that people never learn."

Then she looked up and held my eyes as though she knew even then that it was all going to happen again.

I heard in the village of an occasion when Ibu Suri had gone in the middle of the night to the house of Pak Darus, an old friend who also lived alone, and insisted that he leave his home immediately. She said she had dreamed of a storm which knocked down the ketapang tree beside his house and killed him.

Darus was a very independent old man and, seeing the lagoon still perfectly calm, he had told her she was a foolish woman and far too old to creep around visiting men in the night.

She used several terrible epithets in the old language and stalked off in a fury.

Two hours later there was a sudden storm and the huge tropical almond tree fell right across his bed; but old Darus must have taken the warning seriously, because by that time he was sleeping outside on the veranda and was quite unharmed.

The event caused more consternation in the village than I would have expected. I didn't understand why until I was more familiar with Islamic beliefs.

Muhammad himself said that Allah gives five things to his servants: their dwelling places, their portions, their actions, their travels, and the duration of their lives. And that all these things are decreed and immutable.

The imam felt that the falling tree was an act of Allah, that it had been meant to kill Darus, and that it was unreasonable and unholy of him to have avoided it. On the following Friday his *chatib*, the preacher Marduk, deviated from the usual fixed formula for the sermon that follows prayer at noon, and condemned Pak Darus and Ibu Suri for tampering with Allah's will.

There was a small section in the community who felt that Ibu Suri's dream was also part of the divine plan and that Allah had wanted Pak Darus to be warned, but this view never gained much ground.

The issue turned into a confrontation between the younger

orthodox Muslims and the older people who still held some of the traditional animist beliefs that had been such a strong part of island life before the arrival of the present imam from Java. They defended their contemporaries, but I found the argument they used surprising. In my eyes, the dream was the strange and exciting part of the story, carrying a warning of an event ahead of its time. But for them the storm was far more important. They felt it was Ibu Suri's anger with Pak Darus that had produced the storm and made the tree fall on his empty bed as a lesson to him, and that Allah, powerful as he undoubtedly was, had had precious little to do with any of it.

The old couple took no part at all in the argument, which went on for weeks without resolution. It ended only when Pak Darus decided not to rebuild his home, but to move up to Desa Langit, the original "sky village" on the slopes of Gunung Api, where the old traditions were still valued. Ibu Suri went on with her life as usual, dancing and teaching and brushing her long gray hair in the shade.

By the time I arrived on Nus Tarian, the rift had not really healed, and Ibu Suri wasn't doing much to help it by performing a strange proprietary dance down on the beach whenever a storm raged out on the lagoon. I spoke with her whenever I could, but it was only when I discovered that she also had Tia's facility for hearing in color that I began to connect sensory blending and precognition.

Precognition means knowing in advance. It implies that effects sometimes precede their causes in a way that makes nonsense of the logic of science. But perhaps the strangest thing of all about it is that physics does not in fact forbid the transmission of information from the future to the present. It happens all the time.

If you run an electric current through a system for a while and then suddenly cut it, several things happen, and the actual blackout is the last of these to occur. Two precursor waves go out ahead of the cutoff event. One of these travels, as all electromagnetic waves do, at the speed of light. The other is almost as fast, but is slowed down a little by the properties of the medium through which it passes. And then finally, at a very much slower speed, the event itself arrives. Signals about what is to happen thus actually go out ahead of the happening.

Imagine a missile in flight. It is detected by an early-warning system which transmits information about it to computers that calculate its trajectory and decide it is aimed at the heart of London. Warning sirens are set off and Londoners know that they have four minutes to take shelter. But an antimissile system is also activated; at the last possible moment a vast energy screen is erected over the city, and the missile bounces off to explode harmlessly somewhere in the North Atlantic. An event, predicted by information that preceded it, has not in fact occurred. A tree falls without killing anyone.

The future can be predicted without being predetermined. The biggest problem we have with precognition is a personal one. We are so used to causality, cause preceding effect, that we accept it as a fact of life and have trouble believing that it is not a law of the universe.

Two top theoretical physicists, Harold Puthoff and Russell

Targ of the Stanford Research Institute, suggest that the hologram principle which has been demonstrated for space also operates in the same way for time. That just as each point in space contains information about the whole of space, so each moment in time holds information about all time. In other words, the present is a product not only of the past, but of the future as well.

If this is true, then significant events disturb the area of space-time in which they occur and make waves which move out in all directions. And as memory of the past seems to be far more common than memory of the future, the waves probably move mainly forward in time. There is, however, a backlash, which is more or less apparent depending on the size of the event and your proximity to it. The "significance" of an event would seem to be assessed by its relationship to individual consciousness. The effect of an event on space-time varies according to the number of individuals touched by it. And any one person's chances of experiencing the event in advance increase if it is dramatic, if it concerns them directly or harmfully, and if it is due to take place nearby and soon.

Predictions of death and disaster fit this model well, but it is possible that we all have quite frequent, and completely overlooked, experiences of precognition.

Visualize yourself moving along the time axis of a space-time pond at a slow and regular speed. An event takes place somewhere ahead of you, producing waves on the pond. The closer you get to the event, the more likely you are to feel the waves and pick up information about it. The waves travel at the speed of light and pass much too fast to make sense, but imagine that they interact on the way with the waves you yourself are making. The result will be an interference pattern that moves more slowly and gives you time to appreciate its detail. You begin to perceive the event in advance, but it is not actually happening in front of your eyes, so you decide that it must be a memory. You experience it in your mind, the waves pass by and when the stimulus stops, you subjectively forget it.

Then you reach the point where the waves originate. The event takes place. You recognize it and think, This feels familiar; it has all happened before. It has. That is *déjà vu*—a phenomenon that happens to almost everyone, often several times a day.

Everybody experiences the precursor waves. All that it takes to become a prophet is the ability to keep the information they contain in your conscious mind after the advance pattern has passed you by.

This may be easier for some people than for others. I believe that the sensitivity which makes it possible for some individuals to detect high-frequency electromagnetic signals coming from a distance in space will also help them to pick up information coming from a distance in time. Those who hear in color are more likely to see into the future. But it is worth remembering that each of us is a fragment of the space-time hologram. We all have access to the necessary equipment and can probably learn to use it.

Perhaps it is necessary only to admit the possibility of functioning in this way. More and more it becomes apparent that we can make whatever we will of reality. New and enlarged concepts of how things are, make it possible for us to interact with them in new and exciting ways.

The Bugis who came in with Abu were pirates, direct descendants of those who have sailed and plundered on the Banda Sea for centuries. They came to Nus Tarian for pearls, and whatever else took their fancy.

I noticed that several of the unmarried girls in Kota Rendah vanished while they were there, sent up to the relative safety of Desa Langit for the duration. I didn't know whether to feel flattered or insulted that the islanders hadn't bothered to take the same precautions on my arrival.

Tia stayed, and on their last night she danced for them.

Or rather she danced, as always, for the spirit of the dance, and they and we were privileged to watch.

Kerosene lamps were put up on the trees around the guest-house, and the visitors sat on benches brought down from the school.

The performance began with Pak Moudhi, the island's *kepala adat*, or chief of tradition. He was a marvelous old man, thin and wiry, with a thick white moustache and a brow wrinkled in permanent surprise. He came on wearing a woven kain and a white scarf wound into a turban, carrying two magnificent old kris daggers with jeweled handles. He brandished the wavy blades in our direction and then laid them crossed on the ground, symbols of the island's power and status.

Then two other men came on, similarly dressed, one carrying a huge flat stone and the other leading a child I had never seen before. He was a young boy about four years old wearing just a loincloth and with the sides of his head shaved to leave a band of hair down the middle like a Mohican.

Pak Moudhi positioned the stone behind the daggers, stood the child on it, and then three times lifted him off the ground while dedicating the young boy's life to this occasion and in effect offering him as ransom to future goodwill between Nus

Tarian and the Bugis. The visiting captain went forward, pricked his finger on one of the sharp kris points, and made a small bloody mark on the child's chest. The pact was sealed.

Then the music started.

Once again that jangling chord struck like a blow, forcing the breath out of your body.

It was followed by a new rhythm. A baffling, broken syncopation of incredible intricacy that was at the same time elusive and masterful. So sure of its own control that it could afford to flaunt part of the pattern at you and then whisk it away in a dazzling maneuver that left you floundering helplessly.

I gave up trying to follow and just listened.

It was like watching the sea.

Tia came in from the side swaying gently like fronds of weed in water. Her feet moved her slowly to the center of the clearing and then became anchored, standing as a living reef does, secure on the skeletons of its ancestors. Her hands began to swim and turn, damsel and butterfly fish dancing attendance on the coral court. She moved, and above us a solitary barracuda hung motionless, taking it all in with a cold-eyed detachment.

And over all this exquisite and shadowy lagoon she managed to spread an aura of lunar awareness. A knowledge that things must inevitably change. That the tide keeps coming in.

She and the musicians brought the flood flowing inexorably over the reef, swirling around the coral community and creeping up the beach.

When the music rose to its final crescendo and suddenly stopped short, leaving the ultimate phrase unsaid, there was only Tia there, kneeling quietly on the sand; but every one of us could taste the salt and feel the pull of the ocean at our feet.

A mile from the village, the shady sand of Pantai Rindang was broken by mangroves at the mouth of the stream that sprang from the hills behind. The trees here marched right into the lagoon, propping themselves up on buttresses and sending carpets of spiky roots gasping up out of the rich black mud for air.

In amongst the roots, the shade was punctuated by a moving patchwork of red, yellow, pink, and aquamarine. Fiddler crabs out feeding, scooping up vegetable soup with little claw spoons. Females eating with both hands, but males having to make do with one, impeded as they all are by an outrageously enlarged claw on the other side. Some males are left-, some right-handed, and a good selection of both were showing the flag. Pulling their colored bows in to the body, stretching them out sideways in imperative gestures, raising and returning them in flashing arcs to the original position. Females impressed and rivals appropriately disconcerted, they drifted back to the serious business of getting enough to eat before the tide returned.

It was here, while digging for clams with Ibu Suri, that I heard Tia's story.

"Her father was of this village and married a girl from Bali, but he drowned at sea just two weeks after the wedding. The baby was born the same day as the eruption of Gunung Agung. We all felt the earth shake here on Nus Tarian, and her mother took it as an omen and named her Tiamat Kutam —'the praised.'

"The mother died of a fever when Tia was only six and the child went to live with her father's father up in Desa Langit. I think she was happy there. The old man was of a great age, but still very clear in his mind. From him she learned all that was good in *adat*, in the way of tradition. He instructed her in the customs and the words of hospitality. He sang her songs of history and showed her how to swim. I saw him often walking with her along the forest paths to the warm springs of Mata Air, leaning on her shoulder with one hand while he gestured with the other, conjuring life up out of the undergrowth. Letting her see lizards where there had been only leaves, producing butterflies from flowers and mushrooms out of stone.

"He brought her to her senses and he taught her how to dream. We old ones still know that way. It starts with simple dreams, with messages so clear she would learn to trust them even though they frightened her a little. It is said that it was she who dreamed of a black giant breathing fire on the night before Gunung Iri, the 'jealous mountain,' spoke for the first time in two generations. You can still see the sign."

She pointed up to the volcano above us, the smaller peak at the north end of the island. Lava had flowed only a short way out of the crater, but it had broken the rim and left a scar which still stood out angrily against the green slope of the cone.

"Then one night she dreamed of her grandfather's death

and was afraid to tell him, but he already knew. He died when she was eight, but not before he had made arrangements for her to live with his youngest son, her uncle Abu, down here in Kota Rendah.

"Abu is a good man. Once a pilot for the Dutch merchants in Flores, he used to bring their schooners safely through the shoals surrounding the pearl banks on Aru. But then his wife died in childbirth while he was still fighting his way back against the southeast monsoon. He gave up the sea, staying on Nus Tarian, taking up trading, and raising the child himself. Tia came to join them four years ago, when Ali was only four, and she has looked after them both so well that Abu now travels again in his prau.

"From Abu she learned the beliefs and obligations of Islam and the prayers that make a good Muslim, but Tia prays with her feet. Like me she is a woman and cannot take full part in the rituals, so she goes her own way. She is also an orphan and spends much time by herself, walking along the beach, sitting and watching the sea. The people sense something special in her and they leave her alone. All except me.

"When she was eight, I started to teach her to dance. *Masja Allah!* She sucked me dry. In two years I had taught her everything I could. Everything I knew except that special thing which nobody can give. It has to be here to start with." She tapped her stomach.

"Oh, Tia has it; you can see it every time she moves; but it is not yet complete. When all is ready, the connection will be made and then you will see! There will be dancing such as this island, this world, has never seen. Dancing of the kind that even I can only dream about. It will be life on another level. Then perhaps we shall have a dance of power, the Maro as it was meant to be."

Ibu Suri's eyes gleamed with pride and magic, but behind them there was something else, an old and secret sadness.

Ever since I arrived on the island I had felt this incompleteness. A feeling of things' coming together, but not quite meeting. A sense of something missing.

I dismissed it at first as part of my own reaction to the strangeness of being there. Part of the timelessness produced by the isolation of the island. I felt like a fish in new and separate waters. A little like a time traveler, or a science-fiction character landing on an ancient planet. I was very conscious of my own cultural bias towards objectivity, of being an observer rather than a dancer. Later, when I began to get involved with the children and became excited by their talents, I thought it might have something to do with the division between the old sky village and the new coastal town, or with the generation gap that set traditional animists against orthodox Muslims. But in the end I knew it was none of these things.

None of the rifts was deep enough to produce that kind of alienation. There were no rival camps carefully drawn up on opposing sides of any of these issues. Everyone was in the same unsettled state. Everyone was waiting for something to happen.

It did during Ramadan.

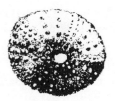

Fasting began with morning prayer on the first day of the ninth lunar month. No food, no drink, no smoking from dawn to dusk each day until the appearance of the first thin sliver of the next new moon.

That year Ramadan fell at the beginning of the rainy season.

The rice had just been planted, and things that had to be done were done without haste during the day; otherwise the people sat around in the shade and talked or listened to the young boys at their recitations in the mosque.

School was closed, and I started taking long walks around Tanah Utara, the northlands, where there were stretches of beach open to a surf set up by the growing northwest monsoon.

Green turtles nested here, and most mornings I would find fresh sign in the sand as though a vehicle on tractor treads had come grinding up out of the sea at high tide, milled around in the dunes, and then made the long haul back to a receding waterline just before dawn.

As the moon grew brighter, there were fewer and fewer laying their eggs, and on the morning it was full, near the middle of the month, I found no tracks at all.

It was a strange day.

There had been a storm during the night, and the early-morning light was still hazy and disturbed. The sea thundered on the reef round the lagoon and crashed against the rocks along the shore.

Ozone was everywhere.

Land people think of it as the smell of the sea, but if you go to sea for long you soon come to associate it with land. It is both and neither. A mark of that marginal world where land and water meet. A region of huge unrest, where only the hardiest or the most adaptable have any chance of survival. A place of change and conflict, of compromise and shift.

That is part of its attraction. The knowledge that nothing there remains the same for two days in a row. That and a deep fascination with old battlefields. With places where we fought to gain a foothold, where we struggled long and hard, and won.

I wandered along the shore that morning, turning over driftwood, rooting in patches of stranded weed, and tuning in to the dismal cosmic hiss in empty shells. My eyes were on the ground, my world restricted to the sand around my feet, so I didn't see what lay at the end of the beach until I was nearly there.

It was almost too big to see.

More than thirty feet long and taller than I, a huge, sleek blue-gray mound with a series of humps and ridges tapering away to a flattened tail.

A sperm whale!

Still alive, but not alone. Tia was there with it.

As I ran towards them, the whale heaved and blew a hoarse breath, struggling to fill its lungs against the unaccustomed weight of the huge body on land.

Used to diving more than two thousand feet down into the deeps in pursuit of giant squid, it was now, for some unfathomable reason, stranded in just six inches of water.

It seemed to be a young whale, probably one of the many immature males that form loosely knit groups peripheral to the pods of females that gather round an old bull in the tropics.

It was possible that the storm had produced turmoil that resulted in confused underwater echoes which led him astray, but nobody knows exactly why hundreds of whales every year cast themselves in an almost suicidal frenzy onto sandbanks and beaches all over the world.

This poor young male didn't seem to understand what had happened. He struggled to move, but succeeded in doing little more than raising his tail flukes and smacking them down on the sand with a hard, sharp sound and sending spray shooting out behind him.

It seemed to be impossible for him to lift his huge square head off the ground, where it almost concealed the small underslung lower jaw. We could just see a line of teeth between white lips and the edge of his bright purple tongue. And behind and above the angle of the jaw, a strangely small and very desperate eye with a panic rim of white showing all the way around the dark iris.

The whale seemed to plead for help or explanation, but there was nothing we could do. The tide was still going out.

I thought that fifty or sixty men might be able to refloat him when the water returned, so I went back to the village, leaving Tia standing there with hands pressed together at her throat and tears running down her cheeks.

In Kota Rendah I ran into an unexpected problem. Everyone was excited about the whale; some of the older people remembered when the same thing had happened once before at exactly the same place, and the whole community was anxious to help.

They didn't eat whale meat and they couldn't understand the extent of my concern for a "fish," but they were perfectly willing to do whatever I thought best.

Or at least, Pak Hashim and the people were until the religious authorities arrived.

"No. I forbid it. It is unlawful and unclean," announced the imam.

"The Quran forbids it," added Chatib Marduk, and he then went on to quote chapter and verse. "Forbidden unto you are carrion and blood and swine flesh. And all dead save that you make lawful by the death stroke."

"But the whale is alive," I pleaded.

Marduk drew himself up to his full height. He was not a big man, but he had a face like that of a bird of prey and a voice that cut like talons. "You are *not* an Indonesian. You are *not* a Muslim. You do *not* belong here, and you will *not* interfere."

It is very unusual for one of the people to speak to anyone, let alone a visitor, so directly.

The effect of this relatively minor tirade was correspondingly enormous. Everyone stopped talking and stared.

I knew that all the goodwill and friendship given me over the preceding weeks were being put at risk by this confrontation. I tried desperately to find a way round it.

"Saudara Marduk, you know a little of me. You know of my respect for your traditions and of my love for your children. You know of my interest in living things. I have no wish to interfere with the customs of the people. Only a desire to show mercy for one that suffers."

I could hear the beginning of a buzz of agreement and sympathy around me and was encouraged to add, in Arabic, a phrase that opens every chapter in the Quran.

"*Al-Rahman al-Rahim*. In the name of the most merciful."

The imam began to look a little uncomfortable and might conceivably have given way, but Marduk was obdurate. He had committed himself with the outburst.

"The mercy of Allah embraces all things, but he also decrees all things. The law is clear. We may not touch that which is unclean. Not pig's meat, nor any unlawful food. And in this holy month, not even so much as the wet coat of a dog."

It was a hard line and open to debate, but I was in no

position to start a theological argument. I just turned and walked away, and nobody came with me.

The whale was now high and dry. His smooth skin was beginning to patch and blur, turning dark in the sun.

Breathing was irregular and ragged, a labored series of gasping intakes, followed some minutes later by a single protracted wheeze that shot a small hot haze of water vapor and mucus from the blowhole off-center on his brow.

All through the morning, Tia and I carried up water in coconut shells to pour over his back in an attempt to keep him cool. It seemed to help. The eyes that followed us were less alarmed. Despite the imam's warning, a number of the villagers came over the hill to watch, and the children helped form a chain of water-bearers that kept a constant stream running off his skin.

By midafternoon the tide was lapping again at his right flipper, but even when it reached its peak, the water was no more than two feet deep around the body.

At that moment the whale's eyes were just beneath the surface, and he seemed to realize that it was now or never.

He made a mighty effort, lifting his fins and tail flukes as high as they would go, straining the whole spine into a tight arc and then slapping everything down together in what should have been a great leap free of the surface.

But gravity and inertia were too much for him, and after half a dozen further attempts, he collapsed and didn't move again.

We knew then that it was hopeless. He was going to die.

I couldn't bear to watch anymore and walked as fast as I could on round the eastern shore to the bay of Telok Ketjil, working off my anger and despair in physical effort.

By the time I returned it was well after dark, but the moon was coming up behind me and I could see everything very clearly.

I was calm now, but filled with hopeless sorrow like a doctor forced to watch a patient die for lack of the appropriate vaccine.

The whale was abandoned again by the tide and by all the people except Tia, who knelt on the sand beside the massive head and gently stroked his skin. She was singing to him. Singing one of the soft, sad songs in the old language. A song of friends long dead and times now past, of children grown and gone. A sound like a mother's sigh.

I couldn't understand the words any more than the whale could, but there was no mistaking the meaning. She was keeping him company in the dark hours of his long and lonely death. Sitting in for the other whales who, if he had been dying in the deeps, would have borne him to the surface on their fins, helping him to breathe and see, easing his passage with their sympathy and song.

This child, in her innocence, was doing the proper thing.

I in my rage and futility, and Marduk in his righteous propriety, had missed the point altogether. So bound up in the petty intricacies of our politics and technology, we couldn't see that all the situation required was compassion.

Not how to move the whale, or how to move the people; but how to be kind and to keep in touch. A way of reaching out in empathy to the biggest brain on the planet.

I hung back in the shadows and watched them for a while, a child and a whale in communion.

When the song was over, she started another, a popular local ballad about unrequited love, and when I left she was leaning with her shoulder against the whale's cheek, telling him in great detail about the mud-skipping fish that lived in the mangroves on the lagoon.

He died during the night.

I came back at dawn to find Tia asleep on the sand. The whale's last breaths had been clouded with blood from hemorrhage in his lungs, and a large clot had fallen on her forehead like a wound. I carried her back to the house of Abu, where she slept through that day and all the following night.

I didn't see Tia for some time after that because she stayed indoors helping her uncle take stock in his store.

During the days the village went on with its leisurely Ramadan ways, but when the wind turned to the north in the evenings, there was a thin odor of corruption in the air. Nobody said anything about it because it wasn't a big thing. Just a trace that troubled the night air like an invisible plume of smoke. But it was making everyone uneasy. The whale wouldn't go away.

A week later it was much worse, and by the last night of the month it was so bad that few felt like breaking their fast. But still no one would talk about it, as though the first to do so would be condemned instantly to an identical fate.

The next day a storm hit the island, and for hours it raged and blew, knocking down palms along the shore, tearing the roofs off several houses and turning every path into a torrent.

In midafternoon it stopped just as suddenly as it had started, the sun shone, and everybody came out of doors chattering and laughing as though a great weight had been lifted from them.

It had. When I walked on impulse down the long north beach, what was left of the whale had gone.

Ramadan was over, and that night there was singing and dancing in the mosque square. Everyone drifted along there at the same time as though an appointment had been made. Like all the best parties, it was totally unplanned.

Pak Hashim told long, involved, and ribald tales of the old times; Ibu Suri led the *dolo-dolo*, a choral dance that snaked in and out of the houses until the line included almost everyone in the village who could walk; and even Chatib Marduk was seen to smile.

At the end of the evening we built a huge fire in the center of the square and everyone was gathered round it, quiet now and happy just to sit and watch the flames.

Then Tia appeared.

She was dressed entirely in black, with her long hair hanging free, and she crept in like a demon. Like some terrible vestigial monster, dredged up by our collective unconscious out of primeval slime. She slithered and stalked, crouching in front of the fire, eyes bulging and mouth adrool with some awful appetite. Then she lunged at the crowd, sending children fleeing in panic and tears.

This was no sweet twelve-year-old girl.

This was a dark and primitive passion; a larval, savage spirit from the deeps, given form and substance for a moment in the body of this incredible child. She was bereft of all civilization, abandoned to an old power, a thing of brute strength and no clear direction. Raw primal energy.

Then she seemed to notice the fire for the first time and, looking deep into it, to fall victim to its spell.

The beast cowered and crawled and finally collapsed.

We all remembered to breathe again.

She lay there for a moment and then, when Tia rose to her feet once more, the demon was gone.

In its place was a deity—the goddess of fire.

She flirted with the flames, whirling and turning in divine rapture, taking strength from them to power her creation.

She was creating life, giving body to the dust at her feet, adding a spark of soul, breathing on it once and setting it free. Her movements encompassed the passage of the stars, the procession of the planets, the rising and setting of the sun. A tapestry of birth and breath, of life and love, of growing old and dying.

She was Pele, mistress of the living dead, whose home was a volcano. Hands erupting in a flurry of fingers, she was the fire mountain itself; life-giving, renewing and replenishing the soil; death-dealing with her lava and her ash.

By this time every eye in the crowd was raised to the peak of Gunung Api, standing dark and vigilant over the village. When we could finally tear our eyes away from it back to the square, she was gone.

I found myself trembling.

Something had happened to Tia, and it touched us all.

She had always been able to pluck visions out of the air, to give them form with a flick of her wrist, but this was something different. She was no longer re-creating things seen and heard; she was providing substance for intangible mysteries that exist only on the edges of consciousness and reality.

Ibu Suri was right. Further growth had taken place, and a connection had at last been made. Tia was now complete— and she was terrifying.

SECOND STATE

EARTH

The force of gravity acts upon every piece of the earth, but not equally.

It is partly cancelled out by a centrifugal force produced by spinning; it is altered by changes in the spin brought about by variations in atmospheric pressure; and it is tempered by the pulls of the sun and moon which raise and lower the level of the oceans.

The result is that the whole planet is constantly flexing and stretching in attempts to adjust to the changing balance of these forces. This restlessness is manifest in earth tides that move the ground up and down by as much as a hand's breadth in every twelve hours.

Nowhere is this uneasiness more marked than in the tense island arcs of the Pacific, where the edges of several gigantic pieces of the continental jigsaw puzzle jostle each other for the best possible fit.

In Indonesia the stress is acute. Tidal energy con-

centrates there to such a degree that it must be dissipated in bursts of heat that bubble up in volcanic activity, or in deep-seated earthquakes that rattle the archipelago like a string of worry beads.

On the islands, the people live like sailors long at sea, adapting to the movement around them, but drawn close to Earth's presence by constant awareness of the fluctuating rhythms of its being.

STEP THREE

Trees Bearing Fruit

When the southeast monsoon blows itself out and the rain-bird has been heard, the people clear rice fields of old stubble and prepare for new planting.

First the women take ash from the hearth of every house in a coconut shell and sprinkle it in the fields.

Then several sawahs are flooded with water carried from the well, and seed rice is taken from its store. The oldest woman in the village stands at the door of the granary, and the seed passes from her hands through those of all the elders and onto huge trays, which are carried in procession out to the fields. There the women hitch their kains up to the knee and sow the seed as they sing.

Germination takes place quickly, and the people wait for rain..

It always comes precisely ten days after the first rising cry of *forfora* in the night.

Then buffalo are harnessed to single-bladed plows and driven up and down through the fields. For days the land rings with the high-pitched sound of men exhorting their teams, willing them to keep on moving through the knee-deep mud, singing to keep up the strain. And at nights the village is rich in earth-smelling air.

When all is ready, the seedlings are planted out.

This is the men's job. They form up in long lines across each sawah, singing the traditional planting songs, and with each regular beat they take a backward step and plant another seedling. Left and right, left and right; young boys running up and down the lines replenishing stocks until it is dark or the job is done.

As each section is finished, a long banner of bamboo is raised in the center. This is tipped with a trailing strip of white cloth and a palm-leaf propeller, so the completed fields are festooned with flags and throb and whistle to announce the successful start of yet another season.

By the time Ramadan ended, the fields were soft green seas of young *padi*. Life settled into an easy rhythm, and I had time to explore the island.

I never wore shoes on Nus Tarian. Mine had been lost in the storm at sea, and there were none in the store of Abu large enough to fit me. But it never mattered. I needed none on the beach or in the packed-earth clearings of the village, and there was a fine network of paths round the island worn smooth by thousands of feet before mine. I enjoyed those paths, savoring the feel of the earth and sensing the soil directly with my skin. To get to know someone new, you need to touch a lot.

All the tracks were good ones, well chosen, much-traveled, and redolent of people, but there was one in particular that never failed to move me with its magic. Truly a path with heart.

It started on the beach in the lagoon.

For fifty yards it wandered uncertainly through mud flats and mangroves, but then shrub gave way to open parkland

and suddenly the path lost all hesitation and picked up a rhythm and a life of its own.

It was a narrow path, and there were thousands of ways it could have traveled across the coastal plain to the first of the gullies at the foot of the hills. Any of the routes between the trees, across the flats, and round the outcrops of rock would have served as well. Some would even have been shorter and quicker. But none would have been so right.

The path was never more than a foot wide, but every foot was in the proper place. On the grassy flats, it swayed gently from side to side, matching itself to the rhythm of a walker with eyes on the horizon. Nearing a grove of ebony trees, it made a swing round to take in the fragrance and just enough of the shade to ease a traveler's passage back into the sun. Passing by a wall of black basalt, it leaned out away from the pressure of the rock; but where a stone stood alone in a clearing, the path made a point of touching it at a delicate and friendly tangent. It responded to every current in the landscape, flowing over the years into a final form so beautifully balanced that one could follow it blindfold. Many times I returned from the hills in the dark without any difficulty at all. I simply surrendered my feet to the path and let it take me to the sea.

There is no way in which even the most sensitive architect could contrive a path in such perfect harmony.

Things like that have to grow naturally. They come into being as a result of a sort of spiritual engineering that takes place between the earth and those who live close enough to it to feel the rhythm of its breath. Under these conditions, a new structure achieves a form whose lines enhance and enrich, rather than violate, the character of a landscape. Paths, particularly those which lead to places of importance, become smooth and vital arteries instead of ugly varicose veins.

This one traveled to a very special place.

It was Pak Moudhi who first took me there.

I was slow to recover from the time of the whale and was sitting moodily on the sand one afternoon looking at nothing when the *kepala adat* came and squatted next to me. He was smoking one of his usual thin cigarettes of clove-scented tobacco wrapped in bamboo leaf.

"*Selamat siang* Tuan."

"*Selamat siang* Pak."

"Where are you going?"

This is a standard greeting in Indonesia and requires no specific answer, but I always felt bound to make some sort of response.

"Nowhere in particular."

"Aaaah." A very knowing sound, as if I had just given him a detailed account of all my woes.

"Tuan has seen the turtles of Tanah Utara?"

"Yes."

"Well, in the old days the Mother of All Turtles swam here on the waters that covered the earth. She was heavy with eggs and had nowhere to lay them. So she dived down to the bottom and brought up black mud in her bill and red clay in her claws. These she placed on the surface, and she kept on diving until there was an island in the sea. Then she pulled her body out onto the shore, so tired she lay there weeping."

That was a nice touch. The tear ducts of the turtle secrete constantly to keep its eyes from being irritated by salt water, and while it is on land this process continues unabated, so that today's turtles all seem to be crying in sympathy with their exhausted ancestor.

"After some time she roused herself again and began to dig a deep hole to lay her eggs. Thirteen thousand there were, and all of them hatched successfully. The young spread out over the world, but when the time came for their own mating, every one returned to these parts and dived to the bottom, collecting mud and clay to build islands of their own where they, or their new mates, could lay eggs. And that," finished Pak Moudhi triumphantly, "is why we have so many islands here in Indonesia."

I looked suitably impressed with the logic involved, and for a while we sat and watched an enormous metallic-blue butterfly flap laboriously by like a bird without a body.

"You can still see the great turtle's nest," offered the old man, finally casting out the bait he had so carefully prepared for me. "It is a place of considerable power."

The hook was set.

We walked down the beach and then cut off back into the trees to join The Path.

It touched me with its magic right away, and I hardly noticed the passage of the next twenty minutes.

Near its end, the path joined a stream and flowed with it from a cleft in the lava cliff. We passed through this, parting the trailing creepers with our hands, and stepped into a tiny natural amphitheater with steep black rock walls.

Most of the floor was taken up by a pond of clear water. It came from a cave at the back, flowing through a hedge of *sepanggil*, a shrub with clusters of small white cordate flowers that open to reveal crimson petal ventricles. These bleeding hearts are everywhere in the East associated with calling spirits.

I began to get the feel of the place.

"This is Kesarian, the birthplace of the turtles. The womb of our islands. It is the dwelling place of *segamat*, the life spirit, and the center of all that takes place on Nus Tarian. When any of the people are worried or distressed, tired, unhappy, or ill, they come here to bathe in the pool. Then they go into the cave alone to sit with the spirit, leaving their clothes here at the entrance as a signal that they do not wish to be disturbed."

He pointed out a kain and shirt neatly folded on a rock beside the cleft.

We had approached quietly and were talking in whispers. We crept even more silently away.

I returned early the next morning, bathed in the cool water of the pool, and went on into the cave.

It ran for about thirty feet into the hill, ending in a narrow crack from which the water bubbled energetically.

Along one wall was a low bench built of smooth blocks of stone.

There was nothing else in the grotto; no shrine or altar, no offerings or carvings. Nothing but a gentle, powerful presence. A deep, pervading calm which covered one like an emotional balm that soothed and healed.

I sat there for a long time, watching the ripples of light on the ceiling grow and play, losing myself and gaining strength.

I bounded back down that path feeling free and fit, ready to take on anything the day could offer.

All over the world there are special places like Kesarian that, by general agreement, are more inspiring than others. The sanctuary at Delphi in Greece, the temple precinct of Baalbek in Lebanon, the base of Ayre's Rock in Australia, and the top of Glastonbury Tor in England are some of these. They have no geological or geographical features in common, but all have long been prized for their qualities of grace and mystery.

All have become holy places—recognized by shamans and wizards; visited by Druids, bards, and witches; settled by hermits and meditating mystics. Many were decorated with the charms of aboriginal spirits, embellished by the temples of astronomer priests, and finally surmounted by Christian cathedrals.

Their chains of influence remain intact, their messages transmitted through time in some basic biological way that makes them perceptible and valuable to people of all kinds in all ages.

The Chinese believe that their landscape is irrigated by a network of invisible canals carrying opposing currents which they identify as spirits of the white tiger and the blue dragon. Practitioners of the art of *feng-shui* are employed to feel the pulse of these powers and to decide where a house should be built, or a deceased person buried, in the way most likely to ensure maximum benefit and still preserve the harmony of the countryside.

The concept of harmony is vital. Those who live in close touch with their surroundings do not seek to control the environment. The emphasis is always placed on efforts to break down the separation between man and nature, to fit into the system and become at one with the earth and all its products.

Australian aborigines hold that every plant and animal has a center where performance of the proper rituals will release *kurunba*, the life essence, and help support the natural order. They believe that man has a special responsibility in the business of maintaining a harmonious universe and that he can fulfil his obligations best by reference to the "dream-time." This is a kind of timeless mythical past during which superbeings, now identified by totems such as kangaroos or water snakes, traveled from place to place across the earth performing creative acts.

The routes taken by the totemic beings are clearly identified in tradition, so every season a group of aborigines travels along the old tracks that lace the desert together, stopping at sacred centers to perform the appropriate rituals and sing a line of songs telling of local episodes in the history of creation. They decorate their bodies with schematic diagrams of the traditional tracks and inscribe intricate serpentine designs in chalk and red ocher on special sacred rocks. The people say it is spirit energy in the rocks which creates rain and fertilizes plants and animals, and that their paintings and ritual songs merely stimulate the flow.

Many of the landmarks are well known and easily identifiable from old descriptions in songs and dances, and from pictorial representation on sacred boards and decorated spearthrowers. Young initiates, fresh from learning the lore in cult lodges, can go straight out into the desert and find the water holes, trees, hills, and special rock alignments without any further help. For them, each special natural object is the body or possession of an ancient sacred being, still spiritually alive and influencing the present, and the sight and recognition of it reinforces their ties to the land and brings deep emotional satisfaction.

I discovered on Nus Tarian that there is nothing random or haphazard in the original selection of such sacred sites and objects.

On the eastern coast of the island, there are raised coral cliffs which have become eroded and honeycombed with caves.

The ceilings of these caverns are decorated with delicate little half-saucers of gray cement, the nests of *layang*, a sea swiftlet.

During the breeding season, the salivary glands of this tiny gray-rumped bird become hugely enlarged and contain a special protein which hardens on contact with the air. With this, and sometimes a little lichen for reinforcement, they build their nests.

Once each year, soon after the first rains and before any eggs are laid, one of the clans from Desa Langit comes down to harvest some of this saliva. It is their hereditary right, and everyone in the group helps. The men build long rickety ladders of bamboo and twine and send their sons up to scrape the nests off the limestone walls. The young girls rush around collecting the fallen nests from the floor, and their mothers and elder sisters squat at the entrance to the cave, cleaning and sorting the material and packing it into pancakes bound with strips of rattan.

Abu buys these from them to sell to passing traders, who in turn pass them on to distributors, and eventually they may change hands for as much as a hundred dollars a pound. Last in the chain are Chinese restaurateurs, who mix the nests with chicken, pigeon eggs, or crab to produce a superb soup.

I joined Pak Suran and his clan on the day they began their harvest. The preparations were fascinating, but by the time they began work, the dust in the caves was unbearable and I wandered off to explore the shore.

On that open coast there is always intriguing jetsam along

the tideline. Driftwood, net floats, jellyfish, pumice, cowrie shells, bottles without messages, Portuguese men-of-war, American aerosol cans, and Japanese light bulbs. I spent hours combing through all these riches and, when the sun was high, took shelter in the shade at the foot of the cliffs.

At my feet I found a stone.

It was about the size of a football, black and smooth and irregularly shaped, a little like an abstract sculpture by Arp or Brancusi.

I imagined it was a "bomb"—one of those projectiles formed when solid pieces of rock are shot through liquid lava in the throat of a volcano and expelled with great force to cool rapidly in air or sea.

I set it up on a pyramid of sand and watched it while I rested.

I really enjoyed that rock.

When the time came to leave, I discovered that I had become so attached to it that I couldn't bear to leave it behind. I am not a hoarder by nature, owning very little and having no need to build security by accumulating possessions, but I had to have that strange stone with me. It was quite heavy, but even the weight and the thought of the long walk back to the village were not enough to deter me.

On the way, I stopped at the caves to say goodbye to the nest collectors.

Pak Suran's mother was sitting quietly outside in the shade, and when she caught sight of the stone under my arm she looked hard at it, scrambled to her feet, and came rushing over to me.

But even in her excitement she wasn't going to let me get away with anything less than the complete traditional ritual.

"*Selamat sore*, Tuan Guru. You shall be blest."

"Greetings, Ibu. You shall be blest."

"Where are you going?"

"I go to my house."

"*Hai!* To do what in your house?"

"To prepare my meal."

"Blessings on your meal."

"Thank you. I beg leave to go."

"Peace on your going."

"And peace on your staying, Ibu."

"We shall meet again. But Tuan Guru . . . tell me, what is it you have there?"

At last we came to the point.

"Just a stone, Ibu."

"*Masja Allah!* But that is no ordinary stone."

Her old eyes were glowing.

I held the stone out to her, but she took a step backwards and refused to touch it.

Then she put one finger alongside her nose in a gesture of conspiracy and shouted for Pak Suran to come out of the cave. When he did, she was feigning elaborate interest in a package of nests and I was left standing there feeling very foolish with the stone cradled in my arms.

There was nothing traditional about his response.

"*Astaga!* Where did you get that?"

"On the beach."

"You found it, just lying there?"

"Yes."

Ibu Hali cackled with delight.

But by now I was becoming concerned about my find. Their reaction to it made me think I must have raided someone's treasure-house or, at the very least, desecrated a shrine.

Soon the entire clan had stopped work and gathered round me—talking so fast I had trouble understanding, but they obviously wanted to see the stone.

So I built another little pyramid of sand and set it up for viewing. Everyone squatted round and gazed at it in awe.

"Pak Suran, what is it about this stone? Have I done something wrong?"

"Nothing wrong, Tuan. This is something very special."

"Why? What is it?"

"This is more than a stone. It has spirit. I have seen only one such stone before, the one belonging to my clan, but this is certainly another."

"Shall I put it back?"

"I think not. This is a thing that must be discussed. Pak Moudhi will know what to do."

I was escorted back to Kota Rendah by a procession that grew larger and larger as we got near the village.

Nobody offered to help carry the stone, so I staggered all the way there like a paleolithic Pied Piper. Someone went to fetch the *kepala adat* from Desa Langit, but it was dark before he arrived, so the entire community gathered in the school, where the stone was displayed beneath a lamp on my desk.

Still nobody but I had touched it.

Pak Moudhi walked round and round the stone in silence, looking at it from every angle. Then he nodded and said the one word "Segamat," and everyone burst into conversation.

He asked me very carefully where I had found it and at what time. Was it buried? Was I alone? Why had I gone to that spot? What was I thinking about at the time?

I answered as best I could. Then he explained.

"On Nus Tarian there are nine clans, the descendants of the nine families of old. I am of *ikan*, the fish; Pak Suran of *manuk*, the bird; Ibu Suri of *kupukupu*, the butterfly—and so on. Each clan has traditional functions in our community, and when they meet to discuss their business, they gather in the house of the clan elder around a special stone. We call these *batu tampak*, or 'viewing stones,' because they are good to see. But they may be seen only by those members of the clan who are of age or by the women who marry a man of the family. At all other times the stones are kept hidden in a special basket hanging on the wall. Since our history began there have been only nine viewing stones on Nus Tarian, each one handed down from father to eldest son. Now it seems"— and he frowned at me—"that we have ten."

I apologized and offered to take it back, to lose it.

But Pak Moudhi said no, there must be a good reason for this one's appearing now and it was proper that it should be found by me, a stranger without a clan or a viewing stone of my own.

In the discussion which followed I learned that my stone was unlike any of the other nine. None of the men had ever seen more than one, but a few of the women who had married after coming of age, and therefore knew two viewing stones, insisted that all the stones were different. Each unique, of different size, shape, and material, but all instantly recognizable as something special.

After conferring with all the other clan elders, Pak Moudhi reached a decision.

"This is a viewing stone. It must have a clan. In tradition, the finder of such a stone becomes a clan founder. So this is your responsibility."

I was flabbergasted.

I have always been very scornful of travelers, the ones that still call themselves explorers, who never go anywhere without being adopted by a cannibal chief or becoming blood brother to a warrior or two.

Now it was happening to me, and all because I fancied a rock.

I tried to find some easy way out, but could think of nothing until I looked at Pak Moudhi and saw that he was enjoying my predicament.

But he was also obviously holding out some kind of alternative, and once I realized that there was one, it didn't take long to find.

"May I take the stone with me when I leave the island?"

I watched the old man's face cloud a little in disappointment.

"Yes. The finder of a viewing stone may do with it what he pleases."

"Good. You all have your own clan stones and have no need of another. I have a stone and no clan, so I choose to take this one with me. All of you have seen the stone, so each one of you is of its clan, and I shall take a little of each of you away with me too. But as I can take you only in spirit, so too I take a small part of the spirit from the stone. The stone itself I leave here where it belongs, on Nus Tarian, in case it is ever needed again. All I ask of you now is to help me find a proper place to keep it."

Pak Moudhi was proud of me. He glowed with warm, wrinkled pleasure.

The stone was where I wanted it, back in the public domain, and several people now felt free to go up and touch it.

The discussion about housing it went round and round for a while, dismissing the villages, the fields, and all public places. It touched briefly on the spring at Kesarian, it was gently moved on by Pak Moudhi, and then suddenly the issue crystallized around a single idea.

It was obvious.

So the next morning we all went to Namata.

Up on the western slope of Gunung Api, about halfway to the crater, was a small plateau. All around it the cone flowed smoothly down to the sea, but at this one spot was a shelf produced by a single hot radial dike of lava that had burst out sideways when the crater was blocked by an old and solid plug. It was eighty feet wide and less than thirty deep, and crowded onto it were seven huge lenticular rocks.

Each of these vast stone lenses was about six feet in diameter, lying on its side like a discus come to rest. The largest was at the back of the plateau, partly buried in the slope, with a hollow scooped out of its leading edge to form a worn and comfortable throne. The remaining six were arranged in a rough semicircle around it on the outside of the shelf. It was difficult to say whether or not the stones had been shaped by hand. They could have been natural formations, but had clearly been hand-picked and equally certainly brought to that spot for some deliberate and special purpose. Blue sandstone has absolutely no business being on a volcanic island in the middle of a coral sea.

The people knew nothing about the purpose or the origin of the stones. Namata was a name without meaning, and not even Pak Moudhi knew who had first used it or why. I noticed that there were small offerings of rice and flowers on one of the stones and was told that this one was considered to be important for pregnant women, and that despite the disapproval of the imam, many people came here to pray.

We had come to find a home for our stone, but nobody was sure of the proper form, so we improvised a simple ceremony. Pak Moudhi announced to the assembled rocks that they were about to have company, that a relative had been discovered and that he would personally be very much obliged if they would look after the new infant. Ibu Hali wrapped the stone in a sleeping mat, a hole was dug right in the center of the plateau, and our *batu tampak* was laid to rest. Then we all left, promising to come back soon.

I did.

I visited Namata often, always sitting, as I am sure one is meant to, on the central throne surrounded by rocks and looking out across the lagoon.

From that height, the shallow waters are a catalogue of blended blues—indigo, hyacinth, damson, turquoise, sapphire, mulberry, peacock, and aquamarine. Round the edges of this palette, where the atoll meets the sea, the raised reefs and islands stick up like blunt fingertips. And you are the artist; you hold it all there at arm's length and fashion it at will. You have direct access to an unlimited source of power.

It is a wonderful and terrible feeling.

I toyed with it frequently, going up to Namata because, I rationalized, it was a good place to watch for the elusive green flash.

On certain evenings, when there are no clouds and you can get a long clear look at a distant western horizon, you may see a strange pyrotechnic effect. At the moment the upper rim of the sun touches the horizon, long red waves of light have already set and most of the orange and yellow are absorbed by the atmosphere. If there also happen to be inversion layers of warm and cold air overhead, and if these are sufficiently disturbed to produce turbulence that scatters the short waves of blue, indigo, and violet, then only green is left. And this shows as a vivid and disturbing flash. Blink and you miss it; catch it and you feel inspired and transformed.

One evening when everything seemed perfect, I went to Namata with high hopes. I was certain the flash would appear, and it probably did, but I was thwarted by having the sun set directly into the tiny crater of Chuchu, the little granddaughter cone out on the far edge of the atoll.

About ten days later the conditions again were ideal and I went up once more, expecting to find that the earth had carried on with its customary seasonal tilt and that the sun would now sink clear to the south of the cone. It did set away from Chuchu and I saw the green flash, but to my surprise the sun was once again touching the horizon north of the little volcano, right back where it had been almost a month earlier. I had forgotten the date. It was early in the new year, we had just passed the southern summer solstice, and our star was returning to the Northern Hemisphere.

From that day on, I kept notes. On the date of the equinox, when day and night were of exactly equal length, the sun set right over a mound on Pulau Pandjang, the longest of the coral keys at the far end of the lagoon. And for several days, when the sun was as far away from Nus Tarian as it could get, I learned that it went down directly behind a tall standing rock called Gigi, the canine in a set of raised coral teeth on the northwestern limit of the reef.

Namata was a giant sundial, a huge rock calculator set like the rear sight on a monumental rifle aimed directly at those points on the horizon where the three most significant events in the solar calendar took place. And at each of those distant points stood one of three landmarks on the reef. The *only* three conspicuous landmarks on the entire reef, and one of these was man-made.

Atolls make ideal solar observatories. People who live on them have long horizons; they can always see the sun rise and set. And depending on their location on the coral ring, they see it either coming up or going down against a curved and distant scale graduated by recognizable markers such as palm trees or coral heads. Each observation point has its own set of references, but every observer has everything necessary for keeping an accurate calendar.

The situation on Nus Tarian was made a little more complex by the fact that a secondary eruption had thrown up a new volcanic outcrop at its eastern end. Nothing was visible from the island that could be used to graduate a sunrise, and the western reefs were scattered and submerged, leaving very few outstanding objects on the horizon for taking sunset bearings. And yet the few that did exist seemed to have been used for this purpose, because someone at some time built a facility at the only spot on the whole island where all the markers would be perfectly aligned.

Namata wasn't just a shrine, a small place for making magic. It was a temple.

Certainly pregnant women could find comfort and reassurance there, but the structure itself was clearly dedicated to some more universal concern. It had cosmic relevance and seemed to be evidence of the early existence on Nus Tarian of a people who understood the mechanics of the Solar System and went to great lengths to affirm their connection with it all.

This kind of concern was once manifest all over the world. I have walked the long, straight solstice lines etched into the Nazca plains of Peru. I have stood and watched the sun rise directly over the avenue at Stonehenge on Midsummer's Day. I have made my own measurements to verify the orientation of the Great Pyramid at Giza.

I am satisfied that all these structures were created by people who possessed an astronomical awareness and a mathematical expertise that we have only recently rediscovered. But I am unhappy with the manic attempts now being made to deify these builders as masters of an arcane and intergalactic order to whom all the secrets of the universe were known.

They were people. Born of this earth and, like all things living here, imbued with a natural sensitivity to its cycles and rhythms. We all have Earth's measure and, given the spiritual freedom to express this heritage, we will inevitably and comfortably produce designs that reflect our origins.

For instance, the majority of all people in all cultures so far tested find the proportions 1:1.6 to be the most pleasing. So it is not surprising to discover that this Golden Mean forms the precise ratio between the height of the Great Pyramid and the length of its base. And we need not look for an esoteric message hidden in the fact that the relationship of the pyramid's height to the perimeter of its base is the same as that between the radius and the circumference of a circle. These are natural and harmonious proportions illustrated with equal significance by the relationship between the length of Mona Lisa's nose and the spacing of her eyes.

We know that churches in the sixteenth century were deliberately planned according to classical musical intervals. It is a fact that the proportions of many Gothic cathedrals correspond to similar harmonics, and it can be demonstrated that the mathematics of both the music and the architecture can be applied with equal facility to the spatial geometry of our whole Solar System.

They can also be reduced to formulae and arranged in patterns of numbers such as the magic squares that were once a cornerstone of Masonic tradition. We know that these conventions grew from medieval transcendental magic and from the ideas of Hebrew Cabalists and early Christian Gnostics. And it is likely that their beliefs were in turn derived directly from shamanistic origins. There is certainly an almost unbroken line of influence running through all those involved in producing the structures that seem to have such extraordinary cosmic relevance.

I do not for one moment question the relevance, but I am very suspicious of interpretations that turn our monuments into textbooks of cabalistic science, complete with mathematical illustrations of cosmic knowledge, incorporating coded messages from doomed civilizations to the enlightened few of the future.

It is not necessary to stretch everything around us in a desperate attempt to make it fit some elaborate cosmology. There is no need to labor so mightily over abstruse mathematics. To do so is to deny the elegance of nature.

The summit of Wilcrick Hill in Monmouthshire does indeed form the center of a magnificent geometric spiral of earthwork that covers miles of the Welsh countryside. But the unfolding leaf of an embryonic fern takes on exactly the same natural form with no more or less cosmic significance. The old straight tracks and ley lines of prehistoric Britain were trade routes which also show an unquestionable astronomical alignment. But termites in northern Australia build equally functional nest mounds that happen also to be precisely oriented due north and south without being accused of practicing an ancient science of elemental fusion.

There can be no doubt that architects and town planners did use mystical traditions as sources of inspiration. The man who laid out the village of Badminton in England was also an astronomer and a noted Druid scholar, and his design includes streets that fall on solstice lines and avenues that open up vistas to distant steeples. These churches in turn, in accordance with the practice of the early ministry, were built directly on the sites of traditional holy places once marked by pagan temples or ancient rock altars. So today that whole area of Gloucestershire forms a vast linked structure of historical, mystical, and astronomical significance.

Any place in which people have lived for any length of time does accumulate relevant form and meaning in this way. Tracing the pedigree back to its origins can be fascinating, but there are dangers inherent in getting too far involved in esoteric interpretations. Numbers and patterns have an insidious magic of their own which tends to obscure the truth and to divert investigation.

In many instances, I am afraid this is what has happened and that we are missing something very fundamental. Something which should have been obvious, and is important.

After the first visit I always went to Namata alone, but I was never lonely there. Hovering over the throne, whether I sat on it or not, would be a pulsating little black cloud. A dancing swarm of midges, rising and falling in the air, blowing a short distance downwind with each stray gust, but drifting back on station again like a balloon tied to the stone with string.

Many small flies gather together in this way, beating their narrow wings a thousand times a second, forming what Keats called "a wailful choir." They are usually all-male gatherings, and no entomologist has yet fathomed their purpose.

It has been suggested that the sound of the assembly may serve to lure females into their midst, but nobody has ever seen this happen. Sound is certainly important to them. I noticed with the swarm at Namata that my voice disturbed them, producing a confused movement in the group for as long as I continued speaking. It didn't seem to matter what I said to these midges, or in what language, but a fellow biologist in Helsinki says that the G note at the opening of a popular Finnish folk song always brings the local species rushing to his mouth. My pitch is not that precise, but I discovered that a sustained low note would bring the swarm down and that a double note on a rising scale sometimes scattered them completely.

It seems certain that the female wingbeat has a special tone which is attractive to males of her species, but sex is apparently not what brings the clubs of males together in these decisive clouds. Pregnant females congregate in the same way.

On Nus Tarian there is a cluster fly that breeds in buffalo droppings and sometimes gathers in thousands on trees or in houses, for no apparent reason.

One evening I saw such a swarm on the ceiling of the *sarau*, the village mosque in Desa Langit.

The muezzin told me they congregated there for several days every year at that season, and had done so ever since he could remember.

They seem not to be returning to a place marked by a special smell, because this identical spot was chosen again even after it had been painted over since they were last there.

I caught several of the mosque cluster and found they were all females, probably already impregnated.

When I told the muezzin, he collapsed with laughter and finally explained that the imam would be outraged. Women were allowed into the building only under sufferance, and it was certainly untoward to have an entire congregation in that condition.

Working females in a honeybee colony also gather in swarms prior to hiving off to start a new community. Here the congregation has a very clear function. All the workers get together round their queen for a long democratic dance discussion about the respective merits of new nest sites. They gather wherever the migrant queen happens to come to rest, but it has never been discovered why she chooses the places she does. Very often totally different swarms, separated by years in time, will cluster like beards on the same branch of a tree or hang in a seething mass from the identical point on an outcrop of rock.

Fly swarms seem to form not because the individuals respond to one another in this way, but because of a common response to certain landmarks. A single gnat can form a private little swarm of its own in an appropriate spot. Sight seems to play some part in the choice of that place, because I noticed that a gnat which normally hovered over flooded *padi* fields would respond in the same way to the reflection from a light-colored kain laid out on the ground in the sun.

Other species go for prominent features such as bushes, rocks, or even people. The distinctions they draw are surprisingly fine. When two people walk together and then separate, the midges that have been hovering over them often follow one and not the other. And it is not necessarily always the taller one, though the height of a landmark does have some significance. Tall trees sometimes carry an umbrella of flies that can be seen even from a distance. And church steeples, wherever these are available, exert a magnetic attraction for swarms of all kinds in such numbers that they look like plumes of smoke and have often been the cause of false alarms.

Most congregations of normally solitary organisms are easily explained. Vultures circle together in rising columns of warm air because these thermals are isolated, occurring only over hills or open sandy spaces. Swifts weave jagged communal patterns in restricted areas of the evening because it is in these places that they all find their flying food. But what brings the mosquitoes there? Why expose themselves to heavy predation by birds and bats if they gain no reproductive advantage from doing so? There must be a good reason, some powerful attraction to the places where they gather at such risk.

Often there is an obvious focal point, but sometimes swarms can be seen gathered very definitely together in areas apparently devoid of all markers in the form of conspicuous sights, sounds, or smells.

Wild antelope and deer select resting places with great care and attention, but the spots they settle on seem very often to be less secure than others only a short distance away. Cattle in a field choose to lie down in one particular area despite the fact that it offers in many cases no apparent advantage in the form of food, shade, or shelter. They may well be responding to stimuli too subtle for us to appreciate, but it is also possible that we could be underestimating our own sensory capacity. Very often the cattle congregate in that part of a field already selected at some earlier time by man for the erection of a standing stone or the construction of a mound or barrow.

The system works both ways. Braunton church in Devonshire stands where St. Branock found a sow lying with her litter. The monks of Lindisfarne, wandering about the North of England with the uncorrupted body of St. Cuthbert, were led to the site of Durham Cathedral by a stray cow. The architects of Namata may have chosen to put their throne stone on the spot favored by the midges, or the insects may simply have come along later to enjoy that particular new configuration.

The question of which came first is really totally unimportant. What matters is that we share a common sensitivity with many other species and are all able to respond in some way to a set of stimuli that give certain places, and only those places, a necessary, special, and magical quality.

Wherever holy places exist, they are accompanied by legends that tell of their discovery. They are revealed by the performance of a magical rite; they come to light as a result of some divine omen; or they are found because someone has had a dream or a vision. If no account is given, then you can be certain that the new shrine is built on top of an old one, that the chosen site was already one of traditional sanctity, and that the tale of its original revelation will have been one of this kind.

The choice of such places, for settlement or worship, is always the result of inspiration rather than intellection.

Originally, the inspiration fulfilled a need, produced the place, and preceded the shrine. Then with the advent of organized religion, a strange situation arose in which there were numbers of sanctuaries in search of inspiration and a place to be enshrined. The Crusaders had no trouble; they simply knocked down crescents and put up their crosses. The Spanish invaders in South America solved the problem by building their churches on the sites of native temples, and sometimes even by appropriating local festivals and traditions. But all missionaries sooner or later were faced with the problem of finding suitable sites for churches or mosques in areas where no shrines existed. Many sought help from the same source. They used a diviner.

A diviner is someone who discovers the unknown by guess, prophecy, or intuition. In the case of the early Church they were often also divines—priests who had an added ability to discern which places would be most auspicious for religious purposes. From what we know of their methods, it seems that they used both knowledge and inspiration. They studied the heavens and related features in the local landscape to them, interpreting the configuration of natural features in terms of constellations and planetary attitudes. They worked much as astrologers still do, calculating first on the basis of fixed relationships and then applying their results intuitively to the particular situation.

To assess their results you have only to compare the sites they chose with others selected more recently by purely secular considerations. The old ones have a mood and a balance which is unmistakable. They occupy positions of advantage; these need not be prominent in the sense that they straddle the highest hills, but they always lie at the focal point of an area. At a point where physical and spiritual forces combine to produce emotional equilibrium. By comparison, the new sites which are allocated by town planner or municipal architect on the basis only of space available are awkward and barren locations straddled by forlorn and empty halls.

The clerical diviners were geomancers, feeling their way to the right answers and the proper places. Most relied on intuition, but I have seen an illustration of at least one using a mechanical aid—swinging an incensory on the end of a chain held at arm's length as he walked through the fields in search of inspiration. I have a feeling that particular divine was very much in demand, enjoying the same reputation for success as many contemporary diviners do in their search for water and precious metals.

I have worked with several professional dowsers and been able to test their talents in the field many times. On one occasion the employer in search of water was actually the local church—and the dowser was forced to report that the strongest reaction, the most plentiful source of water, lay, unfortunately, directly beneath the church steeple.

Buildings themselves, particularly old ones, produce a

marked response in many dowsers. One I know was able to trace the entire length of a Roman drain, now buried fifteen feet beneath the streets of London, by walking around the area between Kensington Palace and the Thames with his pendulum and a sample of ancient brick.

This talent is proving so useful for archaeology that the University of Toronto has a unit dedicated solely to exploration of this kind.

A dowser clearly needs to be able to discriminate among a variety of signals, but when it comes to situating churches and locating hidden sources of water, it seems likely that the old divines were responding to exactly the same stimulus as the modern diviners.

We know that subterranean flowing water produces abrupt magnetic variations on the surface. Sophisticated instruments that measure minute changes in nuclear magnetic resonance are being produced to prospect for water, oil, and metals in the field. But even the best of these is nowhere near as successful as a human dowser. There is no known physical process that can be used to explain why dowsing aids such as willow forks, whale bones, coat hangers, amber beads, surgical scissors, or brass rods should be effective as amplifiers, resonators, or antennae. Indeed, the very variety of aids suggests that they are in themselves unimportant and that the vital component in these detector circuits is a human being.

Compared with many other natural systems, the human electromagnetic signature has a high frequency, and it could be this which gives us our special sensitivity. Normal sound frequencies on their own, for instance, are not high enough to make much impression on a magnetic tape; so before being passed across the inductive head on a tape recorder, they are first mixed with a "bias." This is a consistent and very high frequency, usually about 70,000 cycles per second, which creates sufficient potential at the head for the lower variable sounds of voice or music to be impressed on the tape. On playback, the bias is filtered out, leaving only the true signal. Our relatively high frequency may act as a similar sort of bias in dowsing. A metal rod or wooden twig on its own cannot produce any marked response to environmental change, but given the boost of a high-frequency human bias, it might be able to respond in some way to the field through which a dowser passes.

In the end, however, the twig and the tape recorder fall into the same category. They are aids which we can do without. We can hear the music, we can feel the signal, on our own. Some of the best dowsers work with their bare hands.

It is likely that we can dispense in the same way with all the new devices now flowering on the fringes of parapsychology. The Hieronymus machine, the de la Warr Radionic Diagnostic Instruments, the Pyramids, and even Reich's Orgone Accumulators all depend on a man–machine relationship. The instruments use a variety of materials and components in special shapes and textures, but all are designed to assist the operator to receive information in the form of energy. They seem to do this with some success; but the machines perform no understood function by themselves, and I suspect that every single one of them will in the final analysis prove to be nothing more than a psychological transfer mechanism. A talent filter or placebo that enables us to let ourselves do some of the things we can and ought to be able to do without assistance.

The pulse of our planet is fast. Earth's magnetic field fluctuates between eight and sixteen times each second. The predominant rhythm of our brain lies in the same area. It is unlikely that this is purely coincidental.

A baby spends the first nine months of its life surrounded

by the steady drumming of its mother's heart. It becomes entrained to this all-pervading rhythm. If at any time in the first
year after birth it is exposed to an identical pattern, it re-
sponds to it by crying less and gaining more weight than other
babies deprived of this contact with their roots. But it seems
that nobody is totally abandoned. We are all biologically
entrained in the same way to the basic rhythms of Mother
Earth—and these are always with us.

And we are all in the same boat. If the natural rhythm of
any biological system is disturbed, it can be reset in the same
simple way. The rate of oxygen consumption by germinating
potatoes, the pattern of emergence of fruit fly larvae, the tidal
opening and closing of oysters, or the body-temperature cycle
in man can all be synchronized once again with the biological
timekeeper by means of a short, gut-wrenching burst of
radiation at ten cycles per second.

I loved the sunsets at Namata and enjoyed sitting up there
on the throne waiting and watching for the flash.

Sunrise was another matter altogether.

I discovered this when one of the waringin, or wild fig,
trees up in the hills was in full fruit.

I had spent most of the night watching huge yellow bats
flapping around it in the moonlight like lost souls, while juice
and guano rained down everywhere beneath the cloisters of its
branches.

I sat on a rock nearby and took it all in until the first streaks
of dawn began to show and the squabbling bats grew quiet
and melted away on their rubbery membranes.

On my way back to the village, I decided to climb up to Namata and watch the first rays of the sun light up the lagoon below.

I sat as usual on the throne, feeling fine and glad to be where I was. Then, as the sky grew lighter behind me, I began to feel uneasy. I walked up and down the plateau until the mood passed and then sat down again just as the sun touched Gigi, out on the reef.

I had been on the throne no more than thirty seconds before nausea hit me as suddenly as seasickness and I found myself on my hands and knees beside the stone gasping and vomiting.

I left the mountain and went back to Kota Rendah, having to stop twice along the route to relieve painful stomach cramps that were producing slight diarrhea.

I had tried some of the figs during the night to see what the bats were making so much fuss about, and assumed that I was now paying the price of that experiment.

I never again ate wild figs, but I did on one occasion have similar trouble at Namata.

Once again the moon was full, and Pak Moudhi had prophesied a partial eclipse.

He called it "bleeding" and explained that once in a while a great but evil hunter passed this way and tried to kill the moon with his spear. Often he hit her and always she bled a little, losing the white light of her power as it ran out of one cheek and let the cold gray skin show through. But never had she been allowed to die completely, because the people everywhere wished her well, praying, dancing, and making loud sounds to frighten the hunter away until she could regain her strength and light once more.

The whole village gathered on the beach near midnight, and thanks to their strenuous efforts the moon did recover and all was well.

After the excitement was over, I didn't feel like sleeping, so I walked south along the lagoon on my own.

Just before dawn I again felt the urge to go to Namata, and I arrived on the plateau about fifteen minutes before sunrise.

As I walked out onto the clearing between the stones, I lost most of the vision in my left eye. A procession of colored dots and lines on a hazy background made me very dizzy, and I stopped for a moment to try and catch my balance. I took a few steps forward, intending to sit and rest on the throne, but such a fierce throbbing pain burst out on the right side of my head that I was almost knocked down.

I retreated to the path, and as I got about a hundred feet down off the shelf, everything returned suddenly to normal. I imagined that I had been climbing too fast and had experienced some kind of blackout, so I rested for a few minutes before returning to Namata again.

The sun was just touching the horizon as I reached the plateau, but the feeling of discomfort was so great that I turned tail and fled, knowing beyond doubt that there was nothing wrong with me.

It was the place that was responsible.

Or at least, that place at that particular time.

Much later I learned that at sunrise in many parts of the world there is a unique electromagnetic transmission. For twenty minutes the earth along the sun line is blanketed by a wave with a frequency of ten cycles per second. Later this fades and falls back to the three-or-four-cycle hum that forms a constant background to our daily lives.

Once again we find that frequency associated with physiology. Can it really be coincidental? In the face of what we now know, it seems far more reasonable to assume that our systems, both planetary and personal, are governed by the same timekeeper. And that it is this which is primarily responsible for synchronizing life in a way that makes it possible for us to identify special objects and to locate special places. And it should come as no surprise to discover that many of those places are focal points which highlight the relationship of earth's topography and structure to other key stimuli in the cosmos. Our sacred sites have cosmic relevance not because they were chosen by superbeings with more than human intelligence and understanding, but because they provide stimuli, often simple electromagnetic ones, to which men and midges can respond.

We call this response worship.

Earth is a tree bearing fruit. And every fruiting body is connected to its branch by a strong stalk of energy. The basic rhythms remain the same, but as cosmic conditions change the earth's field alters in sympathy, and that fluctuation filters down to local levels. Its effects are not everywhere the same, but a body anchored at one point in space will be sensitive to these changes in time. And a moving body changing places within a short space of time will be able to detect the difference in space. Our cosmic baseline, Earth's dominant, or bias, frequency, makes this sensitivity possible.

A sense of the special is very widespread. In Polynesia they call it *mana*. A fine pot can have mana, but this is not simply the sum of the balance and craft that went into making it. If the potter consistently turns out special work, then he may have mana of his own. And if he does, he may be stronger or smarter or more graceful than others; but mana is not strength or brains or agility. There is no difference between the mana in the pot and the mana of its maker or its owner. It simply causes each one to excel in a special way. It is the essence of nature. Like electricity, it is powerful but has no will or purpose of its own. It may come from gods or spirits; or it may be produced by the performance of an appropriate ritual; or it may simply exist.

The Iroquois call it *orenda* and the Algonquin *manitou*. Both see it as something in nature that awakes a sense of wonder or produces a momentary thrill. Sioux and Oglala know it as *wakan*. Anything that becomes endowed with spirit and does special things is *wakan*. The Crow rely for inspiration on visions, or *maxpe*, which give a warrior his special power. In Muslim Morocco it is *baraka*, a holiness that can be found in mountains, in the sea, in the moon, in horses, or in magic squares.

On Nus Tarian it was *segamat*, and it was usually found in stones. The people believed that the power was indestructible, although it could be dissipated if its possessor did the wrong thing. It was also transferable and would give strength and well-being to those who used it well. Their instant recognition of the stone I found seemed proof that it was not a vague concept, but one properly defined and easily identified.

There can be little doubt that all of us respond to objects and places differentially. This one feels good and we build a house or church on it. This one feels uncomfortable and we avoid it or build up superstitions around it. One spot trembles with the energy of subterranean water and we sink a well there. Another glows with a different kind of light and somehow we sense that this is a focal point, a place with relevance to other times and places. A spot with more than its share of hologram fragments. It may happen that birds nest on this node or that mammals choose to give birth here. Swarms or flies congregate above it and a yew tree on the site grows tall and strong.

Slowly we learn to appreciate the qualities that make such places recognizable. We take note of the signs, label them auspicious, and look for others like them. We find others and become aware of hidden connections between them. We discover similar properties on a smaller scale in some natural objects. We learn to create comparable forms and relationships in our music, art, and architecture.

Gradually a network grows, patterns fall into place, and old mysteries begin to make new sense. Often we conceal the sense from ourselves by cloaking it with symbols or burying it deep in some obscure mythological construct. But it persists and gets handed down to new generations with new agreements about the nature of reality. The sense remains obscure until new eyes with a different kind of vision once again become aware of the pattern. Arguments arise about the validity of the data and opinions differ. Some reject the designs as coincidental and some attribute them to omniscience, but both polar attitudes obscure the simple, harmonious, natural magic of it all.

We are in tune, and given the chance, we do things tunefully. We dance.

Pythagoreans and medieval magicians evolved operating methods that prepared them for moments of perception. Eastern mystics and adepts of the various forms of trance induction put themselves in positions in which revelations can come more easily. But no information is the exclusive property of any sect or system. There are no stores of knowledge jealously guarded by Masonic or other hermetic groups. There is only natural knowing, and no matter how you come by it, it is the same in the end. You get a glimpse of the imagination of nature. You become gloriously entangled in the web of the universe.

This is our right in Earth's estate. It is our inheritance.

Tia had found her way.

The sperm whale seemed to provide a bias frequency that lifted her onto a totally different level.

It was as though she had been through an initiation ceremony or eaten from some forbidden tree. She had knowledge in addition to power, and for the first time with her I became aware that both could be used for good or evil.

She had always been intriguing, but now she frightened me too. She had become a woman.

Tia still spent a lot of her time on the shore, but no longer so often alone.

With the advent of the unpredictable and often violent northwest monsoon, the island fishermen seldom ventured far from land, and one or more of them were always busy on the sand, mending nets, making traps, or repairing outrigger canoes.

Tia's favorites were two young brothers, Sumo and Ahmad, who had inherited a leaky old boat from their father and were busy building a new one. Most evenings I would find her watching them as they worked. They had cut a section of trunk from a fallen monkeypod tree and dragged it down to the beach, where they had hewed out a rough canoe shape with small adzes. Now they were busy burning out the interior to give the wood a fine, weathered finish.

Ahmad was very big for an islander, slow, and good-natured. Sumo was younger, but sharp and ambitious. He had lived in Sulawesi for a while and loved to talk about his time there. He enjoyed questioning me about other places even more remote, but most of all he got a kick out of discovering that there were things about his little island that I didn't know.

"*Pukul lima*, the name of this tree. You know why?"

"No." The literal translation was "strike five," but I couldn't imagine why.

"This tree is more intelligent than my brother Ahmad here. It can even tell the time. Every afternoon at exactly five hours, the leaves fold themselves up like the pages of the Quran and prepare for sleep."

"Without waiting for *maghrib*?" asked Ahmad. We all laughed. *Maghrib* is the evening prayer.

The monkeypod is one of the mimosa family and like many of them has tiny fernlike leaflets with some power of independent movement.

I went to watch one the next evening and found he was right. One hour before sunset, the huge umbrella canopy seemed to thin out as I stood beneath it, moving almost visibly to show more and more of a clear blue sky overhead. And as the leaflets folded, they released drops of water trapped on their upper surfaces to produce a fragrant and very isolated shower.

"When it is time to return to shore each evening, the boat will let us know by simply closing up and sinking." Sumo grinned at the notion and carried on branding the hull with an iron he kept red-hot in a small bucket of charcoal.

"Tell me, Guru, how do you think we stop the boat from sinking?"

"Speak softly to it, or use an outrigger," I suggested.

Sumo shook his head. "No, we have a better way. When the boat makes its first sea voyage, we will have the imam bless it, of course, but just to make certain we will work something of our own. There is an old custom. For all the time we are at sea on that first day, Tia here and three other young girls, only the most beautiful ones, will sit in a row in my father's house. All day they will sit there without moving. And the canoe will sail steadily and never turn over."

Tia nodded as though this made perfect sense.

It sounded all right to me too. Naturally you make a boat as well as you can, but there are bound to be things beyond your personal control, and having four lovely young girls working hard in your interest makes a great deal more sense than a lady in a flowered hat swinging a bottle of champagne.

I was still lost in contemplation of this notion when Sumo dropped the hot iron on his foot. He screamed and ran down to the water, using words I had never heard on Nus Tarian before. By the time he emerged and hopped back onto dry sand, there was a livid red burn line on the upper surface of his instep, visibly swollen and already beginning to blister.

Even had I had a first-aid kit I knew there was little I could do for him, but Tia was not tied to the same restrictive logic. She lifted Sumo's foot by resting his heel on her right palm and then very gently she placed her small left hand over the wound. He winced as she touched him, but then relaxed slowly. As I watched him, his face cleared of all pain and he looked down at her curiously.

Tia gave a small strange smile, and when she took her hand away, all trace of the burn was gone.

Lights in the Firmament

The imam didn't like it.

He could find nothing in the Quran or the sayings of Muhammad that actually forbade healing, but he felt sure it was wrong.

The recitation, however, is quite clear in the matter of obedience. "Men are in charge of women," and Tiamat would have to stop if he said so. On the other hand, her mother and father were dead, and the fundamental law of Islam is very strong on the care and protection of orphans.

It was a grave problem, and whenever the imam was faced with a difficult decision, he tended to eat and sleep a lot and leave things to his preacher.

Chatib Marduk was a local man, but he had studied in Java and returned to Nus Tarian twenty years before when his fat and worthy superior was appointed by the new authorities in Djakarta. More than the imam, he was aware of the strength of *adat*—of island tradition and custom—and of the importance of giving the sanctity of law to as much local usage as possible. Marduk was building himself an empire, and he was too canny to get involved on either side of an issue until he was sure which way it was going to go. So while he glowered in concert with the imam, he said nothing, and life went on. For several days after the event of the burn, nothing much happened.

Sumo made certain that all heard about it, and almost everyone had either looked at or touched the foot in question. But hearing about something, and actually seeing it happen are different things, and many of the people were of two minds about it. After all, Sumo had lived in Sulawesi, hadn't he? And who knew what people there got up to these days?

Like Marduk, they waited for the next step. For nobody, not even the most skeptical, doubted that there would be further developments. They had all seen Tia dance on that memorable night at the end of Ramadan.

What happened next was very simple, and very complex.

Every village has an idiot.

In Kota Rendah it was Naum, a thin, hyperactive man in his thirties who would get excited to the point of euphoria by small, sometimes totally invisible things.

Once or twice a month, usually between the first quarter and the full moon, he would be seized by a sudden vision too grand to tell, and go capering wildly through the village or down along the beach with his eyes bulging and his hair standing on end. At other times he was depressed and confused and couldn't sleep. He spent the long nights alone, usually sitting on the wall that surrounded the courtyard of the mosque carving vivid and alarming things out of pieces of driftwood, using an old knife with an ornate copper handle.

The people left him very much alone.

Naum never harmed anyone, and the villagers were concerned only that he might one day injure himself with his knife. He was allowed to come and go as he pleased, even taking part in prayers in the mosque. It was there, and at noon on a Friday, that Naum finally reached his twin pinnacles of ecstasy and despair both in the same moment, and it was too much for him.

The men were standing in long lines, all facing west, hands raised to the shoulders, thumbs on the lobes of their ears.

"*Allahu akbar.*"

Then with hands folded in front, the first sura of the Quran.

"In the name of Allah, the compassionate, the merciful. Praise be to Allah, lord of the cosmos."

Naum, standing on his own at the back, began to fidget.

"The compassionate, the merciful, king of judgment day. You alone we worship, only You we ask to help."

He tore off his cap and crammed it into his mouth.

"Guide us to the straight path, the path of those You favor. Not of those who cause You anger, nor of those who go astray."

The men bowed from the waist. Naum fell unnoticed to his knees and began to sway from side to side, keening softly to himself.

"Allah is great."

They stood erect again, leaving him down there alone, banging his head on the cold cement floor.

"Allah is great."

The men sank to their knees, palms on the floor, and pressed their foreheads to the prayer mats. Naum crawled to a pillar and managed to claw his way up it to stand uneasily on his feet.

"Allah is great."

The men came up out of the great prostration and sat back on their heels, and then as they went down again, Naum screamed with his hands pressed to the sides of his head as though both eardrums had burst simultaneously.

Only Marduk's voice carried on with the raka: "There is no god but Allah, and Muhammad is His messenger."

Everyone else turned to look at Naum, who was staggering along the portico, knife in hand, slashing out at a terror no one else could see.

He reached the ladder leading to the minaret and went up it almost without touching. Out on the balcony, he screamed again and again and again.

Alone now in the mosque, Marduk stood, turning his head first over his right shoulder and then over the left, ending his prayer with the blessing "Peace be on you and the mercy of Allah."

But there was no peace for Naum.

Round and round the balcony he backed away from himself, alternately screaming defiance, hacking at the air in panic, or crouching and whimpering in pain.

By this time most of the village was milling around in the mosque square, wondering what to do.

Pak Hashim climbed slowly up the ladder, but came down very much more quickly when one of Naum's wild slashes ripped the shoulder of his *kebadja*. Nobody else tried.

Some of the fishermen went to fetch a net, either to capture him or to catch him when he fell, because Naum was now teetering on the edge of the narrow wall round the balcony, hovering over a thirty-foot drop to the terrace.

He was still wavering there, eyes wild and unseeing, protected only by an atavistic sense of balance, when Tia arrived.

She went straight to the ladder, lifting her hand in a gesture of reassurance when Pak Hashim tried to stop her from going up. She had some difficulty climbing in her tight kain, but eventually she reached the balcony and stood there very still in full view of Naum and everyone below.

For the first time since it had begun, Naum responded to

something outside his personal hell. He continued to scream, but he screamed at her. "Go away. Leave me alone. Why are you trying to destroy me?"

Tia still didn't move, but she began to speak to him softly and clearly in the old language.

Pak Hashim told me later that she was using a ritual he hadn't heard since he was a child, one she must have learned from her grandfather when Tia herself was only six or seven years old.

> Lie awake, lie awake, saying nothing;
> Look for me, I am here, I shout you back.
> My cry is loud, my cry is clear, I call sea eagle;
> Run away, far away, your time has come.

She repeated it again and again, each time taking a step nearer to Naum, who had now come down off the wall and stood mesmerized. He tried to raise his hand, the one with the knife, but he couldn't move. Sweat ran down his face and he began to tremble with the effort.

Then she touched his cheek, and he melted. He simply collapsed behind the wall of the balcony, and all we could see was Tia standing there looking down sadly at her feet. She bent, picked up Naum's knife, and dropped it over the side. It clattered on the stones of the terrace, and breath sighed out in a ripple of relief across the square.

When Tia came down the ladder from the minaret, Naum followed her. His eyes were dead, and he walked like a puppet with her across the sand, past the well, and down to the beach. The tide was in, and at the water's edge Tia paused and pushed him forward. Without turning, he walked in up to his knees and then folded up, face downward underwater.

He seemed to be under a very long time, but it probably wasn't more than twenty seconds before he launched out again, streaming water and looking slightly dazed, but with light in his eyes.

Naum stood and looked at the crowd on the beach. He smiled tentatively. The people smiled back. Naum giggled, and a wave of response moved through the crowd. Naum grinned. The people beamed. Naum offered a laugh, and it came out rather high and shaky, as though it were something he had never tried before.

Everyone watched him very closely.

Then Naum burst into a great roar of laughter, a huge sound that flooded out on a tide of release, and suddenly all the others were laughing together, holding on to each other, staggering around the beach, collapsing in heaps, laughing until the tears ran down their cheeks.

Only two took no part in the rejoicing.

Tia had disappeared, and Marduk stood back in the shade of the palms at the foot of the square, his dark face tight with fury.

Perhaps only he and I realized what had happened.

Tia had healed again.

This time it was an invisible ministration—a thing of the mind—and possibly only temporary, but it had been done dramatically, with all the power and authority of *adat,* and in full view of everyone. It would be impossible to stop her now. The people would never allow it.

Her reputation was sealed beyond question that evening when a fisherman who had been out on the reef during the day tending his traps reported that in the afternoon a *babi-butan*, a boar, with red eyes and enormous tushes had come swimming across the lagoon from the direction of Kota Rendah.

Everyone knew there were no wild pigs left on the island.

The people began to seek her out. Sumo's mother was cured of a fever. Two babies were treated for unknown ills and stopped crying immediately. An old man with failing eyesight claimed she had given him back at least part of his vision. And so it continued, gradually gaining momentum as people even came down from Desa Langit.

I was fascinated. I had studied healers and unorthodox medicine in Africa, in the Amazon, and more recently in the Philippines, but this was a unique situation. Tia was just starting, working entirely on her own in the absence of formula or appropriate tradition. The people usually tended their own wounds with herbal remedies, because there had never been a healer on the island. Now she and they were having to feel their way into this new situation.

For me it was like being present at the moment of creation.

At first there was no pattern to her treatments. She did whatever seemed right whenever she was approached. Usually this meant just touching the offending part of the body for a moment, smiling shyly, and going on her way. Talking with as many of her patients as I could, I found that most seemed to enjoy some relief from their problems, and where any change was visible, it always involved an acceleration of the normal healing process. Nothing unique was happening, but all the normal events took place very much more quickly. Sumo's burn healed in seconds rather than days. A tropical ulcer cleared up in days rather than weeks. A wound that would normally have bled for hours stopped bleeding immediately.

We know a little of what is involved in natural healing. Injury produces a disorganization of electrical patterns, and this triggers an alarm system which brings in squads of white blood cells and antibodies. When tissue is damaged, chemicals sealed within the cells are released also and initiate an elaborate series of reactions that may involve thousands of separate enzymes. If nothing goes wrong, repair normally takes one or two weeks.

Medical practice, both ancient and modern, is directed towards assisting this process by mechanical and chemical means. Wounds too large to be filled by a blood clot are drawn together mechanically by stitches. Infections too severe to be combated by the body's usual resources are dealt with chemically by antibiotics. All this is old established practice; but we are beginning to recognize that electrical, electrostatic, and magnetic stimuli may be even more important, and that all of these could come under personal control.

Self-repair is one of the most fundamental properties of a living system. It is an old and well-established process that can be seen in even the most primitive organisms. In fact, many of them seem to be much better at it then we are. Cut a planarian worm in half and it grows itself a new head or tail. Sever a salamander's limb and it promptly regenerates a new one. In their bodies, no cell is too specialized, too proud to go back and start all over again. No matter what happens, the cells in the vicinity of an injury or malfunction simply stop whatever they are doing and make good the deficit. It is impossible to give a salamander cancer.

We more complex organisms have lost this facility because our cells have become unionized. They each have their own special designated functions, and are no longer available for general duties no matter how important these may be for the welfare of the community. But it seems that they can be shocked into going back to work.

Robert Becker at the State University of New York has produced a series of experiments that demonstrate a clear relationship between regeneration and electrical energy. He cut the forelimbs off rats right at the shoulder. Then he introduced a silver wire electrode and applied a delicately controlled current to the stump, giving it a negative electrical charge. This immediately put an end to restrictive practices and induced the specialized cells in the area to become unspecialized. They reverted to their primitive state, available once again for the replacement of damaged or missing parts, and all the rats regrew their limbs.

In other experiments, ulcers have been healed by the introduction of electrodes into the stomach. Bone fractures, which mend slowly or not at all in old people, have been stimulated to rapid regeneration when a small portable power pack is strapped to the region of the injury. The body's own charge, short-circuited by labor disputes or dissipated by tension and old age, has been given a boost by an outside source of electricity. All healthy bodies have the ability to heal themselves, and external sources of help become necessary only when the normal resources break down.

In laboratory tests several recognized healers have demonstrated an ability to induce energetic changes in cloud chambers and high-frequency discharge apparatus. It has been suggested that the marked magnetic and electrical fields produced in these circumstances are themselves responsible for healing. There seems to be a connection, but I suspect that all the varied and fascinating measurements made on healers in action could be illusory to the extent that they deal only with symptoms which may be highly idiosyncratic and have little to do with actual healing. I feel that any really meaningful explanation of what takes place will have to concern itself more with altered states of consciousness and with the way in which different levels of being, other realities, are connected with one another.

At this point we can be certain of only one thing. Healers heal. And they seem to do so largely by getting their patients to sit up and take notice. They prod them into the natural business of healing themselves. Our bodies have the capacity for doing this. Under hypnosis, we can make blisters and stigmata appear and disappear on command. The problem is to get those areas of our minds which control these unconscious processes to go along with the scheme whenever we need them. This is the difficult part, and healers have to resort to all kinds of ploys to make the maximum possible impression on their patients.

Most healers have no conscious awareness of doing this, but their techniques often demonstrate an extraordinary intelligence that is far more revealing about the nature of healing than experiments with magnets or mice could ever be.

I guessed that Naum was schizophrenic and I watched for a recurrence of his symptoms, but he seemed a new man. It was as though Tia had managed to nurse him through a dangerous but ultimately benign fever which opened up areas of self-discovery for him. During the days after his last attack, she hovered round and did two things which I didn't understand at the time but which began to make uncanny sense a long while later.

She fed him on fish and clams and, something nobody in the village had ever eaten before, a soup made from the brain of a slaughtered buffalo calf. And she kept custody of his knife until she was certain he could once again be trusted with it, and until she had got someone in the village to replace the copper handle with a new one of carved and roughened bone.

Despite the fact that a quarter of all the hospital beds in

many Western countries are occupied by schizophrenics, we still have no clear idea of what the problem is. Research is going on in attempts to track down genetic factors and elusive biochemical connections. Some workers are even investigating the possibility that certain lines in the palm of the hand may be used to predict schizophrenia and catch it in its early stages. Hormones, diet, complications during pregnancy, and attacks of rheumatic fever have all been blamed, but nobody really knows.

Out of all the work, however, a pattern is beginning to emerge. A schizophrenic has abnormal sleep patterns, an inability to estimate time accurately, unusual brain waves, low blood sugar, a deficiency of vitamin B_{12}, and an abundance of exotic substances in the urine which produce hallucinations when given to normal subjects. Schizophrenics also have abnormally high levels of copper in their blood. This trace mineral is important in hormone production, but if the body has an excess, then an enzyme is activated which produces hyperactivity. And copper can be absorbed through the skin.

I don't know what made Tia replace the handle on Naum's knife; she herself had no clear idea about it; but it seems that she did the right thing.

Neither do I know what prompted her to make brain stew, but there is evidence to show she may have been right about that too. It seems that schizophrenics have a high concentration of alpha-2 globulin molecules. We all have some, and we need them to control a chemical reaction that is vital to the transmission of signals along nerve pathways. But schizophrenics have too many, and this may be why they sometimes experience sensory flooding and occasional psychotic states. The abundance of the guilty molecules is apparently due to failure of an enzyme, but the shattering part of this study as far as I am concerned is the discovery that the enzyme can best be replenished, and this is the method in use in the project at Detroit's Lafayette Clinic, by feeding patients an extract of beef brain.

This extraordinary ability to go right to the heart of a problem, to take action that was meaningful and appropriate beyond her conscious knowledge or control, was to become a trademark of Tia's.

The people marry very young.

While I was on Nus Tarian, a marriage was arranged between Daud, the youngest son of Pak Hashim, and a beautiful fourteen-year-old pupil of mine named Rahi.

Her father, Saleh, discussed it with Pak Hashim, and a bride price of a paired team of buffalo, plus a bull for the wedding feast, was agreed on. The fathers made the arrangement entirely without consulting the young couple, but everyone knew they were lovers and expected it to be a very good match.

The next important decision was the selection of an auspicious date. There must be a moon, since people have to walk all the way down from Desa Langit, and no party in either village was ever given on a moonless night. Pak Moudhi was consulted and agreed that two days after the next full moon would be ideal.

Saleh immediately started to enlarge his house in order to accommodate all the guests, and his wife, Petimo, began to make plans for the celebration. She invited guests by visiting each home with a present of *dodol,* a kind of sticky toffee made of glutinous rice and palm sugar. By this sign, the people knew that the feast was going to be on a grand scale and that appropriate gifts would be expected.

Any guest invited to a meal always brings a *tjupak,* which is a large measure of raw husked rice. But for a feast of this kind *tembaga* were also necessary. These were old Chinese copper coins with a hole in the center. They are no longer legal currency in Indonesia, but in many of the islands they still function as tokens of worth. On Nus Tarian they circulated rather like stock certificates.

Petimo was issuing invitations to all those who held outstanding obligations to her family, and on the day of the wedding these would be honored in numbers of *tembaga.* In this way, money paid out over the year to other people's feasts is called back like a loan. At a big celebration the hosts can even make a profit, with which they can purchase a new net or a buffalo. Nobody, however, wants the surplus to be too large, because then it becomes a liability. Large donations from others would tie them to making corresponding returns at some future date.

Those who were not formally called to the feast would of course come anyway, because anybody's celebration on Nus Tarian was everybody's concern, but they were not expected to bring more than the usual gift of rice.

Three days before the wedding, Petimo summoned a number of women to help in *kerdja,* the work of preparing food.

On the first day they gathered in the shade outside her home pounding spice in wooden mortars and shredding large quantities of coconut.

The second day was given to the making of sweet rice cakes called *nasi kunjit* and of *djalor mas,* long golden strings of syrup and egg poured through a funnel of banana leaf.

And on the third day, the bull was slaughtered and turned into a whole range of wonderful curries that sent beckons of fragrance out to every part of the village.

The wedding began at noon.

As the guests arrived at Rahi's home, they placed their contributions of rice in a huge pot on one side of the doorway. On the other side was a magnificent Sung porcelain bowl, old and cracked around the rim, but still blue as the sky after rain. It was filled with water, and a dipper was provided for rinsing the feet before entering the house.

Inside, each arriving group of six or seven were immediately given personal bowls of rice and access to communal dishes of meat and vegetables cool enough to be eaten by hand. Then sweetmeats and tea were served and we went out to sit in the shade and make way for new arrivals.

When most of the guests had been fed and were gathered there smoking and chewing betel, the *tembaga* contributions were collected. Each man in turn approached Saleh, gave him the coins, and grasped his hand in the conventional greeting. Saleh then spoke the guest's name out loud and dropped the copper coins one by one with a loud ringing sound into a metal bowl. Everyone listened and counted the strikes very intently, like brokers watching the big board.

When all the preliminaries were over, the performance began. Two competing groups of singers started a friendly duel, chanting verses and responses from the Quran, while Pak Hashim and Daud and the rest of their family took up positions of honor for the traditional wedding rites.

Then we all waited for Rahi to arrive.

We waited a long time.

The bride was being prepared for the ritual by her mother and the older women in another house, and when the time came for her to lead the procession out, Rahi couldn't do it.

She collapsed in a rigid catatonic state, with her eyes wide open and every limb paralyzed and stiff.

The people had never seen anything like it.

Ibu Suri came to call me because they thought I might know how to deal with Rahi, but there was nothing I could do. I suggested that one of her own friends might be able to get through to her, and someone went out and came back with Tia.

Tia was clearly frightened by the sight of Rahi lying rigid on the floor, but she took her hand and began to stroke it. Then she turned to us and said one word, "*Susah*," which is an all-embracing term for every kind of pain, trouble, difficulty, and hard luck. It seemed like an obvious and unnecessary comment on the situation; but we should have known better than to judge Tia too quickly.

She rolled Rahi over onto her side and began to unfasten the silk baju the bride wore on top of her new white kain. Rahi's mother made a move to stop her, but Ibu Suri held up a warning hand, and we all watched Tia bare the girl's smooth brown back.

There should have been nothing under the baju, but Tia reached in and pulled up a tangled mat of thorny vegetation.

The women gasped and began to say the word "*Susah*" again; and then I remembered that there was another meaning.

Tia had miraculously produced a branch of what is known locally as *pohon susah*, "the trouble tree."

It is a species of rattan whose leaves end in a long, thin, drooping midrib set with many small, sharp, recurved hooks. These lie in a fiendish tangle facing in every possible direction, and once snagged into fur, flesh, or clothing, they bite deeply and there is very little you can do. Struggling only gets you further and more hopelessly entangled. I have heard it said in Malaysia that this is the only plant on earth that can stop a charging tiger, and I believe it. The only way to get out is to reverse and unhook each barb independently.

As Tia carefully worked the thorns free of Rahi's clothing, I realized what the whole incident meant.

The young bride was terrified of the wedding ceremony and had become paralyzed with fear. She allowed something to hold her back. Tia diagnosed the condition in one word as a "difficulty," but she used a word that has several meanings, one of which describes a common plant sometimes also known as the "wait-a-bit" tree. Rahi had wanted to wait rather than go on with the ordeal, and she had found an unconscious solution to the dilemma.

Tia, in her own astonishing way, provided a perfect way out. She somehow produced a foreign agent, something that could quite clearly carry the blame for holding the girl back. Something that could be taken out, and looked at, and discarded. Something, moreover, that was in itself a marvelous visual pun, a communication in the kind of language that the unconscious mind understands best.

When Tia rolled Rahi over again and waggled the thorn branch in front of her eyes, the girl smiled and sat up and went straight out to the ceremony.

Daud went through the elaborate ritual of the groom without a single hesitation, Rahi sang the bridal song, and the guests danced late into the night by the light of flaring torches stuck into the ground.

It was a lovely wedding.

This was not the first time I had seen a healer use a technique tailored in an imaginative and delightful way to the particular needs of the patient.

On the island of Luzon in the Philippines, healers dramatize their rituals by dressing them up in a way that makes it look as though they were actually going into the body with their bare hands and bringing out all sorts of offending odds and ends. For Filipino patients it is usually sufficient for them to produce banana leaves or bits of coconut husk, objects locally associated with the kind of witchcraft that produces illness. But for foreigners, different productions are obviously necessary. When a Swiss patient was being treated for a stomach complaint, the healer produced a Swiss noodle. Not just any old noodle, but a fresh one of a kind made and eaten only in the canton of Ticino, where the patient lived.

On another occasion, I was traveling up the Amazon in a narrow riverboat with three Brazilian *caboclos* when one of them developed a severe toothache. An abscess beneath a wisdom tooth had become inflamed, and the man had a high fever. I had no appropriate antibiotics, and I battled unsuccessfully to extract the tooth with a pair of the engineer's long-nosed pliers. I was considering calling off the trip and turning back downstream when one of the boatmen mentioned that a healer lived just a few hours up one of the smaller tributaries ahead.

We moved out of the muddy main stream into a quiet pattern of lagoons of clear green water. The mosquitoes and biting flies disappeared, and the air was full of kingfishers and flocks of parakeets. Eventually we reached an area where the forest had been partially cleared to plant a crop of cassava, and pulled in to the bank near a collection of palm-thatched huts.

I went ashore with the patient and saw him seated on a log

in a clearing in front of the home of the healer. In a little while the great man himself came out, and he was a terrible disappointment. He was a small, hungry-looking middle-aged man with little hair and fewer clothes. Just a tattered pair of shorts, plastic sandals, and the remnant of a T-shirt which carried the unlikely claim that it belonged not to this strange man but to the State Prison of Louisiana.

A brief conversation took place in Amazonian Portuguese, and the emphasis, as far as I could understand it, was placed not so much on the patient's symptoms as upon the particular circumstances, the exact time and place, in which they had first been noted. Some sort of agreement was reached which seemed to take the blame off poor dental care and place it squarely on a malevolent outside influence, an evil spirit force which, as it happened, the healer knew well.

He returned to his hut for a moment and emerged with a number of unspecified materials tightly rolled into a ball of greasy black cloth. I was dying to see what it contained, but he simply put it on the ground between the feet of the patient and it was never referred to again.

Then the treatment began. Singing softly to himself in an Indian dialect, the healer pushed the patient's head back until his mouth was wide open. Then he put his crooked forefinger into the mouth and stirred around in there. He grunted once or twice, peered in again, and then reached in with thumb and forefinger and picked out the offending molar as though it had been simply lying there loose under the tongue.

We all examined the tooth and peered into the empty socket, which was bleeding only slightly. There was great satisfaction all round, but the healer wasn't finished yet. He said that he must still get rid of the pain. To do this, he massaged the swollen glands on the patient's throat, then made him sit back again with his mouth wide open.

The healer sat cross-legged on the ground opposite him and began to sway to and fro with his eyes closed. I watched very closely, suddenly aware that this was not just a tired little man in rags, but a very impressive person. Then someone in the crowd hissed and pointed at the patient. A trickle of blood was beginning to flow out of the right corner of his mouth and run down his chin. This was not surprising, but what happened next was something that brought a great roar of laughter from all the observers, but made the hair at the back of my neck bristle.

Out of the side of his mouth, following the line of the trickle of blood, came a column of live black army ants. Not a frantic confusion of ants, running in every direction, as they would have been if the healer had dropped some sort of container holding ants into the patient's mouth, but an ordered column of ants. Ants marching two and three abreast, coming from somewhere and going somewhere.

They kept on coming until there were a hundred or more, moving in a stream down the patient's neck, along his bare arm, down onto the log on which he sat. Then he and I and everyone present watched the column as it marched off into the grass at the edge of the clearing and away.

Thinking back on that experience later, I realized that the healer had started off the consultation by concentrating not on the symptoms of his patient, but on the peculiar circumstances connected with them. He was concerned not so much with how he had come to develop the complaint as with why it had happened to him, and why now, just as he was starting on an important trip. He tried, as all Western physicians will, to give the condition an identity separate from the sufferer, to set it up so that it could be treated. But he was not content with a fine-sounding diagnosis. He went beyond treatment of the symptoms to tackle root causes by suggesting that some outside agency, an evil spirit or some personal ritual deficiency perhaps, was responsible. The cause he came up with may not have been the right one, but by recognizing any at all, and by taking obviously appropriate action to deal with it, he was providing, in addition to his efficient dental treatment, psychiatric therapy at no extra charge.

To me that seemed like very good medicine. The patient was simply given the means to make himself well. And this was accomplished by a superbly judged piece of sleight-of-mind.

When the crowd at the healing laughed at the sight of ants crawling out of a man's mouth, it was not the nervous laughter of people in fear or discomfort. It was honest loud laughter over something that struck them as very funny. I didn't see the joke until it was explained to me later. In the local dialect, the same word is used for pain and for the army ant. The healer had promised that the pain would leave, and so it did in the form of an elaborate and extraordinary pun. It walked out.

For that patient, in his culture, with his expectations and beliefs, the treatment was highly effective. He got better very quickly.

For this observer, in his certainty, with his patterns of logic and procedure, the whole affair was shattering. It took me a long time to come to terms with it. It was years before I could even bring myself to talk of it. Whom can a scientist tell about an experience like that?

But I no longer have that problem. Not since I number theoretical physicists amongst my friends. They have taught me that the objective world in space and time does not exist and that we are forced to deal now not in facts, but in possibilities. Nobody in quantum mechanics talks about impossibilities any more. They have developed a kind of statistical mysticism, and physics becomes very hard to distinguish from metaphysics. And that makes things a little easier for a biologist faced with biological absurdities.

Breaking the rules doesn't worry me anymore now that I can see that only one principle really matters. And that is rightness. If it fits, if it feels good, if it seems appropriate and meaningful, then it doesn't matter how absurd it is in the light of the established explanation of how things work. Establishments are no longer as stable as they used to be. They are having to make way for another kind of knowing which is concerned only with harmony, with keeping in touch with Earth's tune.

When the tide went out, it exposed patches of weed, chunks of coral debris, and isolated pools of water on the flats in front of the village.

Most days the fishermen's wives, some of them with babies strapped to their hips, would be out there collecting for the evening meal. Often I joined them, partly because I enjoyed scavenging for myself and partly because I wanted to know which things interested them.

Mussels, whelks, razor clams, stone crabs, and baby octopuses all went into baskets as often as they found them. Sea urchins at certain seasons and some of the beaded green algae were also popular. And fish when the women could get them.

Most days there would be small snappers or young rock cod caught unawares by the receding tide and trapped in the shallow pools. Two women working together with wooden spears could soon corner the fish against a rock or drive it out in panic onto the sand.

But there was one kind they never could catch, even though it was quite common.

It was a goby. One of a large family of very successful little torpedo-shaped fish with blunt heads that taper away to almost nothing at the tail. Most of them have pelvic fins more or less joined to form a leglike sucker under the body that helps them to hold on to wave-washed rocks or leap across obstacles between the tides.

The species in the lagoon was mottled purple brown, and the women called it "pelompat," the jumper.

When surprised in a tidal pool, these resourceful little gobies jump right out. But they don't leap indiscriminately into the air. They always land directly in another pool, often as far as three or four feet away. And if sufficiently disturbed, they jump again, launching themselves with unfailing accuracy into pool after pool, each one a step nearer the sea.

Every time the women set one off, they shouted "Pelompat, two, three, four, five, six . . . ," counting aloud each leap on an ascending scale that ended in a ragged cheer when the fish either reached the sea or set a new record for the day.

The greatest achievement I witnessed was a traverse of more than fifty feet, making use of no fewer than eighteen separate pools along the way. This performance provoked cries of delight and a ribald comparison between the movements of the pelompat and those of old Pak Darus the day he sat on a wasp.

The topography of the tidal flats was constantly changing, and I was amazed that the gobies were able to keep a clear enough map in their minds to make their moves with such unerring precision. I am certain it is memory that is involved, because they are just as accurate on dark nights, and I found that if I emptied a pool on their route, they jumped right into it anyway.

This was the method I used to catch them, making a grab while they were still high and dry and hadn't yet recovered from their surprise. I was able then to examine them at leisure in a bowl, because they made no attempt to leap out of an unfamiliar pool into unknown surroundings.

On several occasions I went out on an early-morning low tide and changed a part of the landscape by digging several pools of my own. When I returned for the following low tide that evening, I found that gobies used the new pools as though they were old established landmarks. They obviously learned their escape routes at high tide, going over the ground and noting the spots where there were depressions that would become useful pools once the tide went out. And I found they could do this equally well in the dark, because pools dug in the evening were used with the same familiarity early the next morning.

I wondered whether this memory was a short-term one, held only from one tide to the next, so I caught a goby as he used one of my artificial routes and kept him in a bowl for over a week. I marked the route with stakes and made certain it lay along the same pattern on the day I released the fish again. When I put him into the pool at the landward end of the path, he showed some confusion and great reluctance to leap; but when I threatened him he did jump, and finding the next pool where he expected it to be, he seemed to gain assurance and made a faultless and very impressive passage through the remaining seven pools and out into the sea.

This kind of orientation based on memory and a knowledge of the land is not unusual amongst animals. Honeybees remember the location of good foraging grounds for a long time. Continuously dancing bees can even reproduce from memory the distance of these sites and their angle to the sun, and make allowances for any change in solar position. In one instance a bee that visited a particular food source was kept in a closed hive for five weeks and at the end of that time was still indicating the position correctly, making all the appropriate astronomical corrections.

I think that in this capacity for making delicate responses to the environment and keeping them in mind lies a clue to the origins of intelligence and creative awareness.

The ancestors of all big-brained oceanic whales and dolphins lived in muddy rivers and estuaries. There are five relatively primitive species, very much like the old fossil forms, that still live in the waters of the Ganges, Indus, Yangtze, La Plata and Amazon river systems. The species in the Ganges is blind and all the others have very poor sight, depending entirely on echolocation to find their way through the murk and to their food.

During the tropical rainy seasons, the rivers flood and spread muddy water far over the land. The Amazon in July grows from an average of two or three miles to over fifty miles wide. At these times, most of the fish desert the main stream and spread out into a maze of pools, lakes, and channels in the forests where they breed. The dolphins are forced to follow their food, and for several months each year they must live in very turbid water only a few feet deep. It is a magical experience to take a small boat at this time and thread your way in amongst the trees at dawn or dusk. The Amazon dolphin is a vivid cosmetic-pink color and shows no fear, threading its way between and under roots and branches, parting the leaves with its long-beaked face, rubbing gently against the side of the boat, and rising easily in open patches to blow.

During this time in the trees, the dolphins must be able to form and retain detailed topographic maps of the areas in which they forage. When the waters recede they often do so very rapidly, and the dolphins have to make their way back to the river through as much as a hundred miles of tricky territory in a short time. There is no time for following the flow or trusting to trial and error. Fish that do this get trapped, and jaguars and men have an easy time picking them out of drying pools. But the dolphins never make such mistakes. I have yet to see or hear of one's being left behind by the tide.

The making of such a map in the memory requires well-developed association areas in the brain. Dolphins have these, and they seem to have acquired them as a result of the pressure provided by their need to navigate through the floodlands. Later, when descendants of the original river dolphins moved out into the less demanding clear waters of the open sea, this huge mental apparatus was free to be applied to more social ends. They were ideally preadapted for the kind of awareness and communication that seems to have led to high intelligence and consciousness.

I find a lesson in this. I believe it is only through Earth-awareness that we can reach higher levels of consciousness. Without a deep and full appreciation and understanding of your environment, there is no possibility of extending yourself beyond it to a place with meaning and relevance. You need to pick up the pulse and learn to flow with it; otherwise you end up taking a bad trip. You have to be grounded before you can fly.

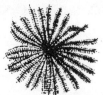

Scattered over the surface of the island, usually in dense thickets of undergrowth, I found a number of extraordinary mounds. They were six or eight feet high, domed, and about twenty feet in diameter. When I came across the first one just a few yards from the beach, I asked about it in the village and was told they were made by a small bird. It seemed impossible, so I chose to find out for myself by lying in wait beside a fresh-looking mound.

Nothing happened for several days.

Then one afternoon just as I was about to doze off, a great commotion broke out at the edge of the clearing. Dead leaves, sticks, stones, earth, and rotting wood began to fly through the air, and backing out of the cloud of dust that moved towards the mound came an untidy mottled brown bird the size of a bantam hen.

He had a narrow face and a worried look, with eyes set rather too close together. His feet were enormous and ended in long curved claws which he used like rakes, hooking up everything in sight and flinging it onto the mound. And all the time he worked, he made a fretful little sound as though the quality of debris these days left much to be desired.

The mound builder apparently goes to these incredible lengths just to save his female the trouble of having to sit on her eggs.

I met her several days later. She was the same size and color as the male, but a little more sleek and a lot less troubled-looking.

When the mountain was complete, she came in and dug a hole in one side and then laid a single very large brick-red egg and covered it over. She left it there to incubate in the heat produced by the decomposition of vegetable matter in the mound itself.

Both parents nevertheless watched over the process very carefully, testing the temperature with their beaks every day and digging up and moving the egg several times, presumably because they felt it was getting too hot or too cold.

One day when I visited this mound they were still fussing about, and when I returned the next day the egg had hatched and the chick was already gone. I presumed that, like quail, the young hatch and walk off immediately.

I asked the children in school about the mound builder and they all knew it well. The birds seem to use the same nest again each year, adding to it as they go along, so the location of all the long-established mounds was common knowledge. I drew a map of Nus Tarian on the board and got them to pinpoint all the locations for me so that I could try to see a hatching actually taking place. We accumulated more than a dozen mound sites, but it was only as I was putting the last marks on the map that I noticed that they all fell into a pattern.

No fewer than seven of the nest mounds lay on an absolutely straight line starting at Batu Jari, the "toe rock" at the foot of the western slope of Gunung Api, and running along the lagoon shore behind the beach past Kesarian, over the hills, and down to the north lands and the ocean cliffs on the eastern side of Gunung Iri.

The line pointed twenty degrees east of north, which did not correspond with the local magnetic variation or seem to be related to the movement of the sun, to the direction of the prevailing winds, or to any geological or topographical feature. And yet it was a very real line, relating most of the mounds to one another in some fixed way.

I never did find out what the relationship was, but when I spoke to Pak Moudhi about it and asked if there were any traditions about the bird or its mounds, he told me a fascinating story.

"Once long ago, when the islands were new, the first people lived in the shade of a waringin tree. The sun in that time was too hot to bear. It shone day and night, for there was no difference then. This was of no concern to Great Turtle and her people in the sea, who could dive down into the deeps if they wanted to escape. But since the turtles had made the land, others had come to live on it and they suffered from the heat.

"The people were dying and they cried out for help. A crocodile passing by on his way to the sea heard the commotion and stopped to ask what was wrong. With his thick skin, he found the sun no problem at all. The people pleaded with him to take a message to the sun asking him to turn the other way. This the crocodile promised to do, but so thick is his skin that there isn't much room for brains inside his head, and he soon forgot all about it. So the sun continued to burn.

"The people had eaten all their food and all the fruit of the waringin tree. Now in their desperation they began to eat the leaves of the tree itself. The very leaves that gave them shade from the sun. They had already started on the first branches when they discovered hidden there a nest on which sat a small brown bird with a long beak. The people were just about to kill and eat the bird when it spoke to them and said:

" 'Wait. I think I can help you. With my wings I can fly to the sun very quickly and ask him to take pity on you poor featherless things.'

" 'But how do we know that you will do as you say and not just go on your way like the crocodile?'

" 'Here, take my egg and keep it safe as a guarantee of my return.'

"So the people took the large red egg from the nest and buried it in the ground beneath the tree and the bird flew off on his mission. The sun was farther off than he thought and he was very tired by the time he got there, but he managed to pass on the message. The sun was most concerned and upset about causing such pain, but he didn't know what to do about it.

" 'If I turn away, the waters will grow cold and freeze. The land will be covered with ice and everyone will die.'

"The bird, however, had a solution.

" 'Suppose,' he said, 'you were to turn away for part of the time, just long enough to let things cool down for a while, and then turn back again later.'

" 'But how will I know when it is time to turn back?'

"The bird thought again and said, 'It would be best if you took a short journey, let us say to the edge of the ocean, and then turned back. That way you will always be facing us for half the time and facing away for the other half.'

" 'But how will I know in which direction to travel?'

"The bird was getting a little impatient and just snapped, 'You will have to use your senses.'

" 'Unfortunately,' said the sun, looking much alarmed, 'I have none.'

" 'Then you shall have some of mine.'

"And the bird pecked once at the rim of the sun and a spark of sight flew off. He pecked again and there was a spark of hearing. And three more times for sparks of touch, taste, and smell.

"So the sun came to his senses and could understand the way. He even came up with some ideas of his own.

" 'I shall leave now and my wife, the moon, shall follow me; but while we are away on our journey the waters and the land will be in darkness, so I shall send my distant cousins the stars to light your way.'

"The bird thanked him and set off to fly back to the waringin tree, but he was still weary from the journey out and his wings wouldn't work very well, so he had to walk most of the way. By the time he reached the people, his feet were so big and swollen that they almost didn't recognize him. They had given up hope, and were about to dig up and eat the egg, when he told them the good news.

"Soon the first darkness arrived. The people went out to celebrate, but they all left in such a hurry they forgot to tell the bird where they had buried his egg. For days and nights as the sun traveled to and fro he searched, probing the ground with his long bill, until eventually he found it. The egg was too heavy for him to fly back up to the nest in the tree, so he decided to bury it again in the ground. But this time he chose a good spot and, to help him find it again, he used his new large feet to cover it with a huge mound of earth and sticks.

"And to this day *timbangwan* does the same."

The name the children had used for the mound builder was *timbunwan*, which literally means "the one who heaps things up." That made sense, but it could have been a modern derivation of Pak Moudhi's traditional name, which meant "the one who balances things."

The more I thought about the old name, the more it pleased me. I began to understand why this indefatigable little bird builds a structure ten thousand times as large as any incubator needs to be. He was *timbangwan,* the balancer, interceding on man's behalf. Stepping in to negotiate a new kind of harmony. A balance between light and dark, between day and night. Setting the sun and the moon in motion and arranging to have them guided by new lights in the firmament. Knocking out the props that hold up the sky in its old static form, but not content just to shout about it like Chicken Little. Offering in its stead the dynamic of a new intelligence. An order governed by the senses themselves, now become wanderers in the form of the five planets visible to the naked eye.

Timbangwan moving things around. Picking up earth here and putting it down somewhere else. Producing balance by rearranging matter into more meaningful forms. Creating harmony by ironing out dissidence and building up power at natural centers. Piling up his mounds in patterns linked by regular but invisible energies. Working towards some great unconscious end, perhaps even controlling the spiritual irrigation of the landscape. Little mound builder making sense by exercising sensitivity.

After I heard Pak Moudhi's story, I came to see the bird with new eyes. I began to understand his expression of perpetual concern. As I watched him probing the ground with his long, sensitive bill, those other mounds on the ley lines in Britain came to mind. I thought of their standing stones, reaching up to the sky, inviting bolts of lightning, channeling the electrical currents of the atmosphere into streams of terrestrial energy. I remembered tales of good and bad energy centers, of places of comfort and places of disease.

Dowsers talk about the connection between cancer and the location of houses placed above "black streams" in which the earth flow has become "sour." They believe it is possible to purify these streams by driving metal stakes into the earth along their course. The theory is that this lets good energies in and an excess of bad ones out. It restores balance in the same way as acupuncture is believed to maintain equilibrium between the complementary forces of yin and yang.

Acupuncture meridians follow the pattern of no known physiological system. They were thought to be purely imaginary until instruments such as the Russian tobiscope were developed to give the lines, and points on them, the kind of electronic reality that science requires. It is possible that this vital current which seems to animate the human body is the same as that which flows through the arteries of Earth. In the cosmology of the Australian aborigines, Earth is regarded as a giant organism in its own right. Many of their rituals are designed to ensure the continued harmonious flow of the planet's vital essences. They take direct responsibility for its health and well-being.

I could almost feel *timbangwan* doing the same. Scraping here, probing there, fussing over the little details in the ritual until everything was precisely as it should be. For a ritual is something in its own right. It is not just something you do, or the words you say, or the place you choose to perform in. It may involve putting earth on a mound or a sacrifice on a shrine, making offerings to spirits or dedications at an altar, swearing an oath or walking barefoot over red-hot coals. The elements in themselves are unimportant because they are not peculiar to the ritual. It is the whole of the procedure that matters. And it does really matter. If everything is right, the parts of the ritual fuse together into a whole which bears no resemblance to any of the components. It becomes a mechanism for folding the abstraction of our reality back into flux where anything and everything can happen.

At a very simple level, ritual allays anxiety. It can resolve tension by focusing attention on some positive and trusted action. When Gunung Api begins to make ominous rumbling sounds, there are only three things you can do. You can ignore it; you can rush to the mosque and pray for deliverance; or you can work magic through the performance of an established rite. Prayer helps, but it is no more than a request. It could be refused or ignored. It is certainly more soothing than doing nothing, but magic is the most comforting of all. Magic is guaranteed as long as you get the ritual right. Everything depends on you.

At the very least, ritual changes those who take part.

Long before Tia began to heal, I watched Ibu Suri treat a wart on the finger of one of her dancing pupils in the traditional way.

The child was sent out into the shallows to find a pure black sea cucumber—one of the starfish's straight relations that has a rather warty surface. This species nearly always carries matching accessories in the form of tiny crabs camouflaged to look exactly like extra lumps on its skin. One of these was discovered, dislodged, and held in place over the offending wart while the child ran three times anticlockwise round the well in the square chanting, "This is your brother *karang*, don't you know him?" Then she had to rush down to the sea and let the crab go.

The wart fell off the following day while the child was swimming.

I believe that ritual can also be responsible for, or at least synchronous with, changes in the environment.

When the *padi* was tall and tiny colorless rice flowers were in bloom, the people held a dance of fruitfulness to ensure that seeds were properly set.

It began at sunset on an old earth platform ringed around with coarse-leaved moonflowers right in the center of the sawahs. Lamps of coconut oil were placed all the way along the path leading out from the village, and a fire burned in the center of the dance floor like a beacon on an island as we made our way there through the sea of fields. Pak Moudhi led the procession, followed by the dancers and by four men carrying an enormous brass gong.

We made a circle round the floor, and the gong was suspended from a bamboo tripod on a second platform a short distance away in the dark. When everyone was ready, the *kepala adat*, stripped to the waist, stood in the center and raised his thin arms to the sky.

There was absolute silence while he reached up openhanded into the night as though he were trying to find something. He turned slowly on his heels and stopped, facing the Milky Way. Now he cocked his head, listening, and all of us strained with him to hear whatever it was he was waiting for.

In the distance, a scattered orchestra of cicadas were tuning up for their evening performance, taking up their song in sequence so that the sound seemed to swell and then fade away. In the *padi* nearby, little climbing frogs puffed out their throats in high-pitched percussion, and an occasional toad contributed its customary discord. We heard these sounds and set them on one side, searching for something else.

I traced the keel of Carina up to the prow at Canopus, then flicked across light-years to Sirius on the breast of the dog, so bright it seemed unreal.

And then suddenly I heard it. I believe we all did.

The far sea-sound of the stars. A white water-light with a silken hiss, sounding and resounding in the sky.

It washed over and surrounded us in a gentle susurrus as we watched Pak Moudhi and waited.

Eventually I saw him tense a little and rise up onto his toes.

Then his head flicked back as if he had been struck, he dropped his arms, and the huge gong crashed like thunder, billowing out across the fields.

The ritual had begun.

Voices chanted a measured tread in the old tongue, and two girls advanced onto the platform, cocking their heads and darting their eyes to accent the rhythm.

Four more pairs followed, and behind them ten young men wearing painted moustaches, making forceful movements with their arms, deliberately strong in contrast to the girls.

They moved into lines opposite each other and then, without warning, the male formation broke up into a wild frenzy of jerks and lunges accompanied by shouts as loud as military commands.

They stopped just as suddenly. The men froze, the shock wave rolled over us, and the soft swell of the women took over again, swaying in time to the chant.

Back and forth the challenge went, alternately brash and subdued as the dancers paraded their power and their subtlety.

Slowly the emphasis shifted as the clash developed from a conflict of opposites into a delicate negotiation between complementary forces.

They began to flirt with each other, advancing and retreating, gradually taking on each other's attributes until male and female became indistinguishable, united in the even flow of a melody that spun a web encompassing everything in the night.

Everything but the gong.

From the moment of the first crash, it kept its own time, booming out across the land at long but apparently regular intervals. The dance ended after about an hour, precisely on the fourth stroke of the gong, and we went in procession back to the village. But the men responsible for the huge brass moonlike disk hanging there over the *padi* stayed on with it.

Throughout the night and all the next day we could hear the gong crashing out again and again, making the air tremble even miles away and sending flocks of white cockatoos screaming into the sky with every stroke.

The beat ended exactly twenty-four hours after it began.

When I asked Pak Moudhi why, he said, "That is sufficient. We have kept the count. Each year we sound the gong exactly sixty-nine times."

"Why sixty-nine?"

"It is the number. It has always been so. One less would be wrong and one more unnecessary."

The ritual existed in its own right and need not have a reason.

I could see that there was no point in probing for further information.

But much later I got some anyway. I learned that the Earth-ionosphere cavity acts as a natural resonator with a period of 1,250 seconds. This means that our planet resounds once every twenty minutes and fifty seconds. We live on a gigantic gong that booms out exactly sixty-nine times every day!

I don't know how the people of Nus Tarian arrived at that magic number, but I do know that Pak Moudhi reached into the sky that night and picked out a sensory cue which he used to set the metronomic ritual in motion. And I see no reason to doubt that the local accentuation of a basic Earth rhythm could have significant effects on growing rice at the critical time of pollination and seed formation.

It is possible that the ritual was devised by a creative ancestor with inside information about geophysical periods. It could also be true that the synchrony is totally accidental.

But I doubt it. Everything in me says no. I see instead an almost incomprehensible mutual interdependence between all matter in our system. I begin to feel the strength of ties that bind our forms together.

Look and you see nothing but rice plants and brass gongs. Feel and you sense a common thread leading back to the same universal ground. Back to a folded order hidden from view but available to sensibility.

The lights that shine so softly through our firmament are the patterns involved in unfolding. Pick out a pattern and you have the key to meaning, the means for healing, and all the help you need to find the way.

Earth lives. Like a great beast it stirs in its sleep, rumbling with internal gases, dreaming and itching a little. It breathes and grows, its juices circulate. The nerves of the world crackle incessantly with vital messages, and now, through the agency of sentient collections of cells on its skin, it begins to feel self-conscious.

We and our planet are reaching for maturity together. Opening up our collective senses to the universe, watching and waiting for the chord that signals the start of a new and even more fulfilling dance.

We are ready to respond to the music of the spheres.

THIRD STATE

WATER

The island is the tip of a mountain peak, rooted in the rhythms of earth, but made even more sensitive by being washed on every side by sky and sea. For there is a dynamic relationship between each drop of water in the air or the ocean and everything that happens everywhere.

Planetary currents move vast air and ocean masses bodily about, redistributing warmth and life, but world news travels very much more rapidly at the interface. Water particles are set in motion by events, going nowhere, but spreading agitation in trains of waves, mingling and interfering, carrying information indiscriminately to every distant shore. When a tropical storm churns up the South Pacific, word of the disturbance soon goes out as turbulence that dissolves in thunder on the beach of Telok Ketjil. There are no secrets at sea.

In addition, each atmospheric pool and ocean basin has its own period of oscillation which reflects events taking place elsewhere. Each time the moon *is full, or showing just a thread of silver as it joins forces with the sun, spring tides send surf leaping at the cliffs of Tanah Utara and brimming over into the lagoon in a flood that carries canoes right up into tangles of morning glory in the dunes. And when one or more of the other planets is added to this alignment, high tides on the sun reach out to trigger changes in our climate, producing downpours that iron out even the roughest seas, leaving unseasonal but meaningful patches of oiled-silk smoothness in the midst of the monsoon.*

We are the products and the owners of a wonderful liquid intelligence. Everything born on Earth is also waterborne.

STEP FIVE

Water Bringing Forth

"Rice is essential," said the people, "but rice without fish is like a day without the sun."

Almost every family owned a boat and had someone who went out line fishing or tending traps; but for regular supplies, everyone depended on the full-time fishermen.

During the southeast monsoon, when the wind was steady and predictable, half a dozen or more outriggers would venture out together each day at dawn and sail sometimes out of sight of land to wherever the terns and boobies hovered over a feeding shoal of tuna or bonito.

With huge hooks and pandanus-leaf lures on the ends of long tarred lines, each boat would work until the load brought its freeboard down to within a hand's breadth of the water. This was the danger line, and anyone tempted by the wish for extra profit to fill the boat any further was regarded as a "three-fingered" or "two-fingered" fool depending on the extent of his greed.

At the evening meal in this season, every house had a helping of firm, fresh *ajoh*, grilled over an open fire, cooked in coconut cream, or simply marinated in the juice of fresh limes. And usually there would be enough left over for a cold snack first thing in the morning.

But in the time of the northwest wind, nothing was quite so certain. The rains came, and only those fishermen who had no fields to tend would venture out in their boats, usually alone, braving waters beyond the reef that could turn from calm to raging storm almost without notice.

Sometimes they would find *pari*, the large ray, or a solitary grouper called *kerapu*. On occasion, shoals of gray mullet would sweep by, pushing their blunt noses along just under the surface in search of vegetation, and those who had and could use the *djala* would bring out their circular casting nets and hurl these out over the water in a beautiful sweeping motion.

Two or three times a year, great multitudes of tiny anchovies took refuge in the lagoon, and then there would be a rush to bring out the one and only *pukat tarek*, a long seine that was communal property. This would be rowed rapidly round the school, and then the entire village would gather to haul it up out onto the beach in a seething silver turmoil.

These were good times, but there were others when everyone had to eat dried fish or make do with the touch of flavor provided by a powerful fish paste called *budu*.

After a long string of *budu* days, the people would grow tired of this dull fare and seek out the *djuru*, Pak Haroun, who was the island's expert on all things to do with fishing.

Pak Haroun grew up on the Kelantan coast of Malaysia, where he learned the technique of finding fish by listening for them. When he came to Nus Tarian, he brought with him not only his knowledge, but a complete *pukat dalam*—a gill net more than six hundred feet long and forty feet deep.

On the island he supervised the building of a special boat to work the net. This was a kolek, or moon boat, thirty-five feet long on the water, but narrow, with a beautiful curved contour and high bow and stern pieces that lifted to every wave. It was painted in five different colors, with a soaring feathered wing on each side of the bow and a sculptured floral *bangar*, or crutch, to hold the mast and sails inboard when they were taken down.

The sails were furled most of the time now, because the *djuru* was old and nobody else had sufficient expertise to use his elaborate equipment. But when times were hard and the people came to plead with him, the old man would listen carefully with an impassive expression, then walk slowly out to the hill overlooking the sea on the edge of Tanah Utara and stand there for a long time with a rapt and happy gleam in his eyes. Then he would give his decision.

This time it was favorable.

The wind had blown gently and steadily for two days, the sea was fairly smooth, the moon was in a dark phase, and there could be shoals of fish lying not far off the reef just waiting to be taken.

The moon boat needed a crew of eight in addition to Pak Haroun. Six of these had to be men experienced with sail and oar in a large boat, but the other two were merely extra pairs of hands for hauling.

One place went to Sumo, who always wanted to take part in everything, and I begged and was finally allowed to fill the other after a crash course in boating etiquette: no shoes (I had none), no whistling (I cannot), and no mention of land animals, particularly dogs and buffalo, by name (I wouldn't dream of it).

There was a problem finding six sailors of whom the *djuru* approved, and the count stuck at five until the following morning when another old-timer, Pak Sila, the brother-in-law of Ibu Suri, was persuaded out of retirement.

Then we were ready.

The moon boat was launched at high tide that afternoon with the huge old net already folded on the floorboards. We sailed out past Pintu and moved westward along the reef.

As dusk began to grow, Pak Haroun leaned over the side to look carefully at the water. Several times he dipped his hand in to feel the temperature, and once he licked the moisture from his fingers to make sure the taste and smell were right. But everyone knew that when the time came, he would use his ears to find the fish.

Finally Pak Haroun signaled for the sail to be taken down.

When it was stowed to his satisfaction, he stood up on the prow and took off all his clothes. It was a measured and seemly ritual, with each garment given the consideration it deserved, like a matador getting into his suit of lights, only in reverse. When it ended, the *djuru* stood there, thin and naked, old and proud, looking steadily out to sea.

He knelt and cupped a double handful of water to his face with a ritual "Peace be on you, and the mercy of Allah." He touched the water with his toe and muttered a private appeal to the spirits of fish and old fishermen. Then he disappeared over the side. No longer old man, now all *djuru*, he hung by one hand from the stern with his head and body completely submerged, listening.

Even though we are predominantly visual creatures, we are extraordinarily sensitive to sound. Every moment, as our eyes scan a scene before us, the brain is unconsciously adding to this source of information by using sounds to build up a complex picture of our total environment which includes details coming in, even round corners, from everything else in the vicinity.

As we travel along in an automobile, for instance, with eyes fixed on the road ahead, we still respond to sounds coming in through the open windows. The brain records regular vibrations from motor and wheels and sorts these out from fluctuating echoes thrown back by objects as we pass them by. It distinguishes easily between parked cars of various sizes, between lamp poles and trees, even between the different kinds of people standing on the curb.

We savor incredibly subtle distinctions. Olympic sporting events are measured only to the nearest tenth of a second, but the auditory areas of our brains are capable of detecting the difference between two sound impulses arriving less than one ten thousandth of a second apart. This acuity makes it possible for us to locate objects in space very precisely by turning our heads until the sound or echo from them arrives at both ears simultaneously. Most people can pinpoint even a distant sound source to within several degrees. But not even a blind man with years of experience in bringing signals of this kind back to conscious attention can do so underwater.

Water is denser than air and not only carries sound along four and a half times as fast, but destroys our directional ability altogether. On land, sound enters the air-filled ears first because it flows around the barrier of the head, which is a thousand times as dense. But the difference in density between flesh and water is so slight that it becomes unimportant, and underwater vibrations pass through the whole skull.

We can pick up sounds from much greater distances this way, but having only one receiver, we lose all sense of their point of origin.

Despite this, the djuru lifted his free arm every few minutes and pointed firmly in the direction in which we should row.

The underwater world is far from silent. Added to the crash and swill of wave action and the rattle of loose rocks along the shore, listening devices everywhere reveal an extraordinary uproar. Shrimps stun their prey by snapping their claws together to produce a constant, sizzling crackle that sounds like a rampant bush fire. Molluscs thrum their mantle cavities like distant rhythmic timpani. Whales rumble and squeal through whole symphonic cycles of overlapping sound. And almost every species of fish seems to have its own characteristic call. Some click or grind their teeth; others belch or croak by blowing bubbles. A few rub the bones of their fins against roughened surfaces in the sockets, and many drum with bands of muscles against bladders in their body cavities tuned to the required pitch with air under pressure.

Each species broadcasts its presence and intentions to the expert by a sound as distinctive as the song of a familiar garden bird. Pak Haroun later described the yellow-striped mackerel as making soft lowing calls like contented buffalo cows. Groupers, he said, croaked with the voices of toads, and anchovies rustled with the sound of wind in dry fronds of coco palm. His training enabled him to identify all the common species, to estimate their numbers, and even to listen in between their calls for the warning *"peyup, peyup"* sound of a shark's tail sweeping to and fro.

And somehow he was able also to overcome all the limitations to which our sense of location ought to be subject when submerged.

As the *djuru* directed, we rowed.

For about half an hour we zigzagged along outside the reef, and then he put up his hand with fist clenched in the signal to stop. He came to the side of the boat and said, *"Selar,* many of them, just here." He pointed.

We handed down the first section of net, and he arranged it as we rowed very slowly round in the direction he indicated, beginning to form the big circle of the gill.

Eventually the net lay in a huge broken ring, and the *djuru* motioned to us to sit quietly. He put his head under again and listened for a long while. He paddled along the line of floats and then stopped to listen again. He hissed angrily and flopped with extraordinary agility, like a seal, straight back into the boat.

We dropped the triangular float at the end of the net and rowed rapidly out away from the opening until we stood a hundred yards off. The *djuru* slid over again and came up shouting almost as soon as he touched the water. We all began to shout and beat our oars against the water and the boat, then rowed a little closer to the net and made another great commotion. Finally the *djuru* was satisfied, and we rushed in and closed the circle.

Then began the long business of hauling.

Pak Haroun started a measured chant dealing with the formidable sexual prowess of an archetypal fisherman called Nik Rung, and at each conquest we recovered another section of the net.

As the circle contracted, the surface of the water began to boil. There were indeed fish in the net, and we could see even in the dark that they were *selar*, a speedy kind of caranx or jack, one of the tastiest fish in the sea. The old expert had not only arranged a meeting with the fish—a clearly specified kind of fish—but had managed to stop them from running.

In the words of the people, it was a clear case of *ikan suka orang itu*—of "fish liking the man." This man, who became a fish the moment his head went underwater.

Dolphins, when they first went back to life in the water, faced our problem with hearing in that medium. Since underwater sound is received through vibrations of the whole skull, ears are ineffective and unnecessary, so they lost them. The auditory channels were reduced to tiny pinholes or plugged with stopples of wax. In addition, whales and dolphins developed hollow jawbones and a great melonlike protuberance on the forehead, both filled with a thin oily substance, much less dense than water, that once again channeled sound to their left and right eardrums as effectively as air-filled ears on land.

Diving man has none of these advantages. He hasn't had time to evolve them. Divers in ancient times sometimes carried oil in their mouths, and it is generally assumed that they did so in order to release it beneath the surface when their work was disturbed by troubled waters. But they may have been more interested in hearing signals or locating warning sounds. I tried taking great mouthfuls of coconut oil before submerging over reefs in the lagoon and it did seem to make me very much more sensitive to sound, but I disliked the taste too much to carry out any conclusive experiments. And anyway, it got me no closer to an understanding of Pak Haroun's oil-less sensitivity.

Dolphins rely on their oil channels for precise echolocation, but sound still impinges on all parts of their bodies with the same high energy and turns every inch into a functional sound receptor. It is not just the surface which is involved either, because sound passes easily through the skin and muscle and bounces back only from bone and air-filled cavities. The internal workings of all bodies about him are a normal part of any dolphin's external environment. When you swim with one, he is constantly aware of your health and general well-being, of the state of your physiology and the level of your emotional arousal. There is no hiding or lying, and no possibility of denial.

It is a rich and wonderful environment underwater, and despite our lack of the dolphin's evolutionary refinements, I believe it is one from which we are not precluded. In fact, each one of us has already been through an intensive training course in all the required skills. Remember? We once spent nine months at the end of a breathing tube, completely submerged in the liquid world of the womb.

There we listened with all our growing being. Surrounded by the steady drumming of a mother's heart, syncopating with our own faster beats, floating, rocking, dancing to the rumblings of the bowels around us, reacting to the creak of joints, the grind of teeth, and the soft explosion of each mouthful of fizzy beer. We could feel each phoneme of speech or song, and through at least the last months of the immersion, we may even have begun to learn our mother tongue.

At a clinic in Paris, children who are still speechless at the age of three or four are being treated with womb sounds. Each child listens in a soundproof room to its mother's voice recorded by a contact microphone placed against her abdomen. To an adult ear, this "womb-filtered" speech is a meaningless blur; but it takes the child back to its liquid origins and allows it to retravel part of that early route and retrieve lost balance and sense of direction. Many react by suddenly beginning to talk intelligibly for the first time in their lives.

We are all water babies and grow into adulthood with many of our original faculties still intact. Pak Haroun kept his talents alive by undergoing a rigorous retraining as a teenager, and even in old age, when his hearing in air was clearly failing, his body sensitivity underwater remained essentially intact. He proved it again that night—and saved our lives.

There were more fish in the net than we could carry.

We took a full load and released the rest. They swirled away, re-forming into a new depleted school as we shook them free from the last knotted sections of the gill.

Pak Haroun insisted on washing the net free of blood and

all trace of the fish immediately, and when several sections became entangled, he went back into the water to free them.

When the job was almost done, he lifted his hand again, abruptly signaling for silence, and still clinging to the net, he ducked his head under the surface and hung there motionless for a long time.

He surfaced in a flurry and scampered back into the boat.

Someone said something about a shark, but he shook his head and began hauling the remainder of the net in as fast as he could, heaping it unceremoniously on top of the fish in the well.

"Faster," he shouted. "We must leave. Now. Something comes. I don't know, but it is very dangerous. A wave I think. We must get back inside the reef."

He was so obviously shaken that nobody questioned him further.

The sail was hoisted, but there was now no wind at all. We tumbled into our places, extra oars were produced for Sumo and me, and we all began to pull as hard as we could for the island and the distant gateway into the lagoon. It was almost two miles from where we lay.

Pak Haroun drove us mercilessly.

Before we were halfway there, breath burned my throat as though the air had been drawn from a furnace. My arms were like lead, but the way the *djuru* was looking out over his shoulder into the dark kept me moving.

When we were only two hundred yards from Pintu, Pak Sila collapsed over his oar without a sound, and the rest of us would have stopped if the *djuru* hadn't jumped down and taken his old friend's place so quickly that scarcely a stroke was lost.

We passed the gates and still he kept up the pressure.

Now that we had reached the familiar shallows of the lagoon, the fear he had inspired in us out there in the dark beyond the reef began to dissipate, and we slowed down.

The lights of the village were coming into view around the point, and the beach couldn't be more than five minutes away.

But we almost didn't make it.

One moment we were rowing steadily along in five feet of water; the next we were standing still as the lagoon rushed by us with a loud hissing roar until we were solidly on the bottom. Several square miles of water had vanished in a matter of seconds as though someone had pulled out a vast plug and drained it all away.

We were surrounded by a silence made terrible by the realization that it shouldn't be there.

I remembered being aboard an ocean liner and feeling the same sense of loss when it broke down completely and the constant throb of all the life-supporting systems suddenly ceased.

Now I had to reach for the missing accompaniment; and when I realized what it was, I knew what had happened.

The breakers had been stilled, there was no sound from the reef, and nothing could suck all that water away from the coral ramparts of the island unless it meant to return it with interest in the solid, hurtling wall of a seismic sea wave.

Deep ocean trenches beneath the rims of moving plates of land are places of disturbed and uneasy equilibrium. Every now and then one of them buckles and warps, sending shock waves racing out through the water overhead. These "tsunamis" travel at speeds in excess of four hundred miles an hour, and in the open ocean they are virtually invisible, cresting a few inches high and about a hundred miles apart. But when they run into shallow water and feel the pull and drag of the bottom, their speed slackens, the wave form steepens, and the height increases abruptly. By the time such a wave hits the shore it may be traveling at only sixty miles an hour, but it can be a hundred feet high, passing completely over islands and leaving the remains of boats stuck up on hills and housetops.

When the wave hit Nus Tarian it probably wasn't more than thirty feet high. But it was still a swirling, seething mass strong enough to pulverize the outer wall of the reef, leaving it in great piles of coral rubble. If our boat had been out there, it would probably have been smashed in the same indiscriminate fashion.

As it was, we were very lucky. The wave spent most of its strength on the reef and came into the lagoon only as a surge that swept us helpless and appalled right over the flats, up across the beach, and headlong into the coconut plantation.

We came to rest impaled on a stump in the dark.

For minutes no one spoke. Then we all began babbling together, taking stock of the situation and our miraculous escape.

Only then did we notice that Pak Sila was still lying exactly where he had fallen when he let go of his oar.

We lifted him out onto the ground.

I could feel no pulse and see no sign of breathing, so I got Sumo to press down at regular intervals on his rib cage while I tried mouth-to-mouth resuscitation.

But we got no response. The old man was dead.

Kota Rendah was protected by its headland from the full force of the wave, and only a few houses on the edge of the village had been flooded. Nevertheless, there was considerable commotion going on when we returned. All the outriggers on the beach had been carried away. The buffalo pens were damaged and several of the beasts were missing. The villagers all were rushing around, talking loudly, and nobody seemed to be conscious of the fact that the moon boat with its nine occupants had yet to be accounted for.

They remembered with a rush when we appeared. There were glad cries of welcome and many questions—stilled almost as soon as they began when the people saw what we were carrying.

We took Pak Sila to his home and to his wife. She was very calm. She rolled out his sleeping mat, we laid him on it, and only when she saw him there in his usual place, no longer his usual self, did she break down and begin a high-pitched wailing. Several of the older women took her away, leaving a large number of men crowded into the tiny room.

The imam, Marduk, the muezzin, and Pak Hashim all arrived together to add to the crowd. They examined the body, and when they too were satisfied that Pak Sila was dead, the imam gave the sign for him to be covered over with one of his kains. The *chatib* said a prayer, and then he and the imam ushered everyone out, leaving only the muezzin, who acted as *mallam* to chant and keep vigil for the rest of the night.

Funeral arrangements on the island were simple. At dawn the following day, the body was carried down to the sea by four male relations and thoroughly washed. It was returned to the house, anointed with sandalwood oil, and wrapped in a new white cloth shroud.

Friends and relatives then began to arrive to pay calls of condolence, and each left a small gift in a bowl at the door. The men, led by Pak Haroun, who felt personally responsible for the death, all gathered in the back room discussing Pak Sila, remembering his qualities and his achievements. The women, led by Ibu Suri, grouped themselves around the widow outside on the veranda, doing their best to comfort her. And in the front room, the muezzin and the *chatib* took turns offering formal prayers and chants.

The extent of the ritual is always determined by the age and position of the dead person. For a stillborn infant there are no rites of any kind; a young person might be given a short ceremony attended only by the immediate family; but the death of an elder such as Pak Sila involves the entire community, and to provide time for people to come down from Desa Langit and for food to be prepared for the funeral feast, the burial is normally delayed until the evening of the second day.

We had to wait even longer than that to bury Pak Sila.

Nobody afterwards could remember exactly what happened.

I didn't see all of it myself, but as nearly as I can reconstruct the events of that evening, they went something like this:

The house of Pak Sila was almost empty of the living.

The men had left to make ready the ceremonial coffin—Nus Tarian has only one, boat-shaped and beautifully carved, which is used to carry all bodies to the burial ground. Ibu Suri had taken her sister-in-law home to help her dress for the procession.

The sun was just touching the horizon out on the lagoon, and Marduk, the *chatib*, replacing the muezzin, now prayed alone and aloud over the body. All over the village we could hear his strong voice chanting, and everybody noticed when it stopped, suddenly, in the middle of a *taslim*.

Several people said later they had heard a soft voice calling the name of Pak Sila again and again, a sound more like a summons than a sigh. Others heard nothing. But every one of those who lived nearby saw Marduk stagger out of the house, moving stiffly backwards through the doorway.

Nobody had ever seen him lose his composure before, and this, almost more than anything else that happened, disturbed them greatly.

Marduk stood on the sand outside, rigid with shock and unable to keep his eyes from the doorway.

A lamp burned in the front room, and everything was apparently as it should be, but nobody was brave enough to face whatever it was that routed the *chatib* so easily.

I arrived at about this time along with most of the rest of the village, and courage grew along with our number, to the point at which several newcomers were preparing to climb the stairs to the veranda.

Then a shadow moved against the wall inside the house,

there were creaks from the old floorboards as something moved heavily around, and a white-shrouded figure shuffled into the open doorway.

A wild, contagious terror spread through the crowd like an electric shock.

It lifted everyone's blood pressure to bursting point, welding us in a single mindless surge of alarm into an organism intent only on fleeing in panic.

But there were too many of us pressed into too small a space for much to be accomplished in that awful moment, and while we still struggled to escape, something else happened that only just managed to prevent us from trampling one another to death.

Tia appeared at the side of the apparition in the doorway, took it gently by the hand, and led the corpse out on to the veranda.

There was another long and terrible moment when our collective sanity hovered on the brink of frenzy.

Then the world came reeling back to grateful reality as the shroud slipped and Pak Sila, thin, brown, and bemused, returned to indubitable life with a muttered oath and a very lively grab that only just managed to preserve his modesty.

Nobody gets used to people's coming back from the dead, but this was a very special dilemma for me.

I have long been aware of the difficulty of determining the precise moment of death. It is widely defined as "the permanent cessation of vital functions," but our methods of measuring these functions are suspect, and even when all of them seem totally to have disappeared, life comes bouncing back from some elusive sanctuary. I outlined this uncertainty in a recent book, pointing out that mistakes are made surprisingly often even by the most skilled diagnosticians with the best available equipment. I said that the errors were inevitable, and would continue to embarrass us, because we were looking for something that didn't exist. I suggested that there was no precise dividing line between life and clinical death. That death was an ongoing process, a curable condition, an integral part of the life cycle, and that the only irreversible changes took place when both life and death together disappeared at a point I identified as absolute death.

I saw this terminal state as one in which organization, which is characteristic of both life and death, finally disappears. And I decided that therefore either matter was alive-and-dead simultaneously, or it was neither, the distinction being drawn by the presence or absence of a coordinating pattern, probably an energy field, which might also contain elements of individual identity in the form of personality and memory. My argument led to a consideration of the present state of our evidence for the existence of such a field. I reviewed several pieces of equipment that seemed likely to bring us closer to an understanding of the field, but I ended by suggesting that in the final analysis no life detector was likely to prove as successful as another living body.

I felt then that our errors were due both to incomplete definition and to an overreliance on mechanical equipment which, even when it functions perfectly, is capable only of fulfilling its designers' limited aims for it. I still feel that our best hope of resolving that dilemma lies in making more profound use of our own underestimated senses.

But my experience with Pak Sila has shaken me to the core.

It suggests that there never was an error. That one can be alive (in the full sense, according to my expanded definition which includes dead areas in a living organism) and one can be absolutely dead at the same time.

When we brought Pak Sila back to the village, I knew he was dead—totally, irrevocably dead, with no hope of recall. My certainty was not based on observations of his pulse, respiration, body temperature, or brain-wave activity. Having none of the instruments to which science usually relinquishes its responsibility, I was forced to fall back on my feelings.

My being was admittedly a little shaken by our experience with the great wave, but I believed what it was telling me. I trusted its judgment of Pak Sila's state, and despite the fact that he subsequently recovered, I still cannot accept this as a necessary invalidation of my earlier assessment.

I think I was right in diagnosing his real and absolute death. I know that I am right about his subsequent state of life—we went swimming together a few days later. And I am beginning to believe that there may not necessarily be any contradiction in all this.

It was the people who set me thinking.

Sumo started it. He had a very simple and logical view of things that tended to involve causes and effects. In this he was very much like all deterministic scientists. He felt that we must have made a mistake, that Pak Sila was never dead at all. But he was the only one who even suggested such a solution.

Everyone else believed that Tia was somehow involved, and

although they were happy for Pak Sila, a lot of the people began to feel rather uncomfortable about having her around.

Marduk had been very badly frightened by it all, and he took advantage of the growing feeling to vent his fear and anger on Tia.

The imam, of course, felt it prudent to go along with him.

But even they never questioned the raising of the dead.

Almost everyone on the island automatically assumed that Pak Sila really had died.

There was concern about the morality and the mechanics of his revival, but nobody doubted that such things could be done.

The islanders were prepared right from the start to accept this nonordinary description of reality, and I began to wonder how much this may have contributed to the occurrence.

Modern physics has a problem. In Newton's time, concern was directed largely at measuring things, because he believed, as many people still do today, that everything was knowable and it was just a matter of clear thinking and lots of hard work. It was felt that the collection of information was vital and that when enough was available, the rest could be calculated or inferred. So classical physics for two centuries concerned itself almost entirely with the motion of bodies and the force of fields.

Then Heisenberg showed it was impossible to determine exactly the position and momentum of any body at a single instant in time. This discovery in itself would have been of only academic importance if it had not also shown that changes were necessary in some of the most basic equations of physics. The changes were made, and they resulted in the development of quantum mechanics, and this has begun to bring about a major philosophical revolution.

Physics is concerned with systems. As an example, let's choose a system made up of a number of moving particles that happen to look like the letters of the alphabet. The old physics had its classical equations of motion which were supposed to be able to calculate the complete state of such a system. Let's say that what they had in mind was an arrangement something like this page of this book. A pattern in code which would need deciphering but which could be used, they thought, like the Rosetta Stone, to understand the language and to predict the form of all future states, the pattern on all pages that might precede or follow this one.

The new physics says fine, but there is a problem. There is no such thing as a single state. Each system has an infinite number of possible states, and it exists in all of them simultaneously. Quantum mechanics recognizes not the page, but the whole book as a more valid expression of the pattern of a system at any one moment in time. In fact, it goes a lot further than this thin book can, because it needs an infinite number of pages.

Now, when we try to observe a physical system, when we attempt to make a measurement, we do not find a particle moving at a number of velocities, located in widely different positions. We catch the system in one of its infinite number of states. When we open a book, we see only one of the many different pages. With the book lying closed on the table in front of you, all those pages or states already exist, and any page is possible. The probability is not necessarily equal; there is usually a bias built into the binding which makes the book open more easily at a well-thumbed page. But with the covers closed, the system is open. It is a multiple state and enters a single state only when a reader comes along to take a measurement or make an observation.

In the words of quantum mechanics, an observer collapses the system into one of its component states. He is not part of the system, he is not one of the letters that make up the pattern on the pages, and he cannot be included in the equations. But neither can he be left out, because without him there cannot be any particular pattern. Without an observer, there is no description; but no description can be considered complete unless it takes into account the effects of the observer who made it. There is no such thing as an objective experiment.

This is the measurement problem, and it has left much of the physics community in a state of considerable disquiet. There are inevitably a number of unconvinced Newtonians (like Sumo) who are doing their best to discredit this interpretation, but so far they have had very little success. The uncertainty just won't go away. In fact, it gets more alarming all the time.

When a system is observed, it collapses into one of its states. But what happens when there is more than one observer?

Science refuses to accept as valid any measurement made by only one person. The experiment has to be repeatable and produce the same result. So when two scientists in widely separated laboratories succeed in making the same measurement, when they get the book to open at precisely the same page, there must be some factor which at that moment puts them on common ground. They must be linked. This linkage, which provides them both with the same page number, is a procedure that we call experimental protocol. It has to be followed precisely or the experiment will "fail"—the book will open elsewhere. It is a very strict procedure with a precise set of rules which require that individuality be held as far as possible in abeyance. It suggests that the scientific approach is a ritual, an incantation, a set of magic words and gestures for producing the desired effect.

And what if there are two observers stationed at the same vantage point? Assume that the two scientists involved in this work happened to be together in the laboratory when the experiment was completed successfully for the very first time. They were exploring new territory, so there was no established protocol; they were simply following a hunch. They collapsed the system and exposed one of its states. Both made the same observation. They saw the same page. This could happen only if the observation process itself united them in some way, or if one of them saw the state first and imposed his view of it on the other. Both sides in the quantum-mechanical argument support the theory of relativity which says it is not possible to put either of the observers first. So that leaves us with only one possibility. Observers of the same state at any moment in time are coupled. And if there are more than two, they are grouped. And as joint observers are often too far apart to hold hands or make any normal physical contact during the process of observation, they must be united by some non-physical factor.

There is only one nonphysical entity that is nevertheless real and sufficiently widespread to be held responsible.

Our consciousness.

Consciousness is experience. It is somehow associated with the functions of the brain, but it is not the brain. There is no instrument, no meter that can make a direct measurement of the conscious experience or decide whether an object is conscious or not. But we have very little doubt about its presence or reality. When you wake from dreamless sleep, when you recover consciousness, you know about it. Consciousness is. It is ourselves, our own personal being. Our self-awareness. But it is also more than that—it involves our awareness of others.

The relation of consciousness to matter may be something like the relation of light to matter. It has been known for centuries that matter influences the motion of light. If objects did not reflect light, we wouldn't be able to see them. And we have long been aware of the principle of reciprocal action—there is no known phenomenon in which one subject influences another without itself being influenced at the same time. But it was not until 1922 that Compton was able to demonstrate his Effect, showing that light itself exerts a pressure and can move and influence matter. Yet in the interim, the reality of light was never doubted.

The reality of consciousness is not in question. And it is obvious that it is affected by the matter of the brain. So the reciprocal action, as suggested by quantum mechanics, is more than likely. There is every reason to assume that our consciousness does affect the world around us, and as that world clearly includes the brain matter of other individuals, our interconnectedness at some level of consciousness seems evident.

Identifying the mechanism is not so easy. Harris Walker, a research physicist with the U.S. Army, proposes a quantum-mechanical theory of brain function in which consciousness becomes possible only when the rate of firing in brain neurons reaches a certain critical level. This is over and above the level of activity involved in unconscious processes going on all the time. And he suggests that in addition to the energy or data rate that makes us conscious, there is another, extra quota necessary to enable us to collapse any system into a single observable state. He predicts that this third value will prove to be independent of physical conditions.

This model seems to work well, and what it means is that there are three levels of organization possible for a living system. An organism can be unconscious, perhaps something like a jellyfish, carrying on a number of complex processes without reference to anything other than self. Or it can be conscious, something like an embryonic human child, floating like a jellyfish in a private sea but beginning to be aware of a possible distinction between self and not-self. And it can be conscious and also exercise this consciousness, by becoming involved in deliberate interactions with other matter. This third level involves discrimination and selection. It is the level of the observer, concerned with the choice of which among many possible states of a system will be the one to become physically manifest. It involves free will.

So if Walker is right, then *will* is the wonder ingredient that joins all systems together.

Pak Sila goes fishing with us.

He is old, and the additional strain of the forced pace of our flight from the wave proves too much for his heart.

He dies.

Our conscious process reaches out to observe him in the customary way. We find something changed or missing, we fail to make the expected contact with his consciousness, and we are disturbed.

We make further observations and, prompted by certain cultural considerations based on our previous experience, we collapse his system into an expected state.

We observe him to be dead.

More than that, if all is as quantum theory suggests, we create his death. It is our will that he be dead.

We then go about our usual preparations for dealing with an individual in that state. Performing acts, making choices that reinforce his deadness.

But we have left a door open.

We delegate direct responsibility for the state of the body to a specialist, to someone who has a vested interest in a description of reality that sees Pak Sila as only partly dead. Someone like Marduk who is paid to, and believes that it is right to, pray for his survival.

The last thing he expects is for the shrouded body actually to revive, to raise its hand and touch him; but his involvement in a dualistic concept of life and death creates a certain ambiguity in consciousness.

Normally this would not be sufficient to change the way in which the community consciousness interacts with an individual system. Dead bodies tend to maintain the defined physical state expected of them.

But Nus Tarian in those strange days was anything but normal. There was a power loose in the land.

Tia had begun to exercise her will.

Our brains respond to sensory excitation. Under normal conditions, input from memory and from the environment is unsynchronized; whole floods of data pour in, and a very high rate of firing is required to meet the conditions set for the maintenance of the conscious state. But if the demands placed on the brain by the environment can in some way be relaxed, then consciousness can be accomplished with less effort.

When a pattern of rhythmic firing, such as the sustained alpha or theta state, is introduced, everything becomes a great deal easier. Consciousness appears at a lower level of excitation and can draw on areas normally set aside for unconscious processes. This is what happens during meditation. There is no net improvement in analytic perception, but conscious experience is expanded in a restful and rewarding way. There may also be another, much more exciting, effect.

As the level of consciousness is raised, the level of the will may also be enhanced. According to Walker's calculations, the channel of collective will is raised to an equal degree, which brings it up to the level of normal consciousness. Will is the factor that selects the observed state of a system, and if it becomes controlled in this new position of strength, it has access to tremendous power. Under normal circumstances it is subject to a certain amount of community control. It is limited to selection of those states which correspond most closely to the current concept of reality. But raised to the level of full consciousness, will is free of the constraints of consensus and can select even the most highly improbable states.

Tia had already begun to heal. She chose to let people be well, and they were well.

She liked Pak Sila and was distressed by his death. It is possible that she simply chose instead to let him live.

This is clearly a bigger thing than healing a blister, but she had help.

The people of Nus Tarian were already closely linked on the ordinary physical level. They had a great deal in common, so it seems likely that they enjoyed a high degree of inter-connectedness at the level of will, where continuity of consciousness is maintained. They were already in agreement on many things and naturally predisposed towards a new and wider agreement about the nature of reality.

Such agreement is a necessary precondition for the collapse of any system into any final state—and the more unusual that state, the greater the agreement needs to be.

So by their way of life and the nature of their beliefs, the island people reduced the normally very high improbability of exchanging a selected state for another less likely one.

Everything was right for a miracle. All the system needed was a nudge.

What it got was Tia, a lonely, introspective child. One capable of operating outside normal sensory limits and trained to respond to rhythms. Someone naturally familiar with meditative states and already practiced in the exercise of heightened levels of will.

With her particular talents and our tacit approval, it happened.

And so Pak Sila lives.

For days on end, my thoughts about all this went round and round in circles. Including an acceptance of other states, other levels of reality, in a formula you have followed for thirty years is not easy. I found myself watching Pak Sila out of the corner of my eye, not altogether convinced of his materiality, half afraid that next time he might disappear altogether and leave me in an even worse metaphysical dilemma.

I walked with him one afternoon along the beach and we talked of many things.

He told me of his admiration for the *djuru* and how he had once begged him to be allowed to learn to listen for the fish.

For months they dived together and listened, but poor Sila could never separate the sounds of the fish from everything else going on down there. The harder he tried, the more mistakes he made.

"I was already too old, of course," said Pak Sila. "But that was thirty years ago and now I am older still, though I am a little wiser now. Do you know what the trouble was?"

I shook my head.

"Come, I will show you."

He walked into the water, and I followed gladly. It isn't often you get the chance to take lessons from someone who has been there and come back to tell about it.

When we were waist-deep, he squatted down and suggested that I put my head underwater and listen.

I did.

The tide was high, but it was a still day and there was no wave action. There were no boats in sight, and the lagoon floor in that area is pure white sand without any rocks or debris. The nearest coral heads were almost a mile away.

It was absolutely silent.

"What did you hear?"

"Nothing."

"That was my trouble too."

"What?"

"I could not hear it."

"Hear what?"

"Nothing."

My doubts about him began to return, but he merely smiled at my concern.

"I could not teach myself to listen to the silence. The *djuru* can do this. He is trained to listen intently to nothing, because the secrets lie in the spaces between the sounds. He is able to listen when all is quiet and to look when there is nothing to see."

I remembered my own interrogation of Pak Haroun and my insistence on being told exactly what each of the fish sounded like. He had made up metaphors to keep me happy, and they had. But now I felt rather ashamed.

Pak Sila watched my awareness grow, and he nodded sympathetically.

A kingfisher swept by overhead, cutting across the lagoon with deep, irregular wingbeats, and it was only in the brief pause between each flurry of feathers and the next that I could be sure of the cool cerulean blue of its back.

Long after it disappeared into the mangroves, I could still hear its loud rattling cry. It is a very distinctive sound which fills my head with the message "Kingfisher calling." But it was only in the silent moment between one proclamation and the next that I had time to think about the bird. It was only in the pauses that I was able to reflect on the relationship between the bird and me.

The silence grew.

I was raised in reason. I was trained in logic and deduction. I am skilled in the art of dividing the world of experience into separate events which are simple enough for me to focus my conscious attention on them one at a time. I tend to review these events in series, looking for cause and effect, even though they may be happening all together at once. This is my bias as a scientist. It makes it possible for me to develop elaborate models of the world, which I can then use as the basis for prediction and decision. It gives me the security of a vast body of information at my back. But it leaves me filled with anxiety. It still doesn't feel right.

My science says, "I see light, because of the sun." But my new understanding suggests it would be just as true to say, "The sun is light, because I see." My consciousness of the sun collapses it into a luminous state, brings it into being. My science puts up a prism and becomes excited by the colors in the spectrum, losing sight of the fact that it is only all together, as white light, that they have meaning. My being needs to be hit on the head before it can accept that silence is a compound of all the sounds in the world.

Natural history began with taxonomy. Its first concern was to establish an elaborate system of classification which gave identity to millions of separate species. Now it has seen the light and is becoming concerned with ecology. It is beginning to be aware of the interrelationships between all those fragments which lie separated in all those museum cabinets. Our Western system of intelligence began by dividing the world into equally fragmentary facts and events. It stressed the integrity of objects and the independence of ideas. It set things apart from one another. But it has always been strangely reluctant to acknowledge the existence of the spaces in between.

Emptiness makes us uncomfortable. Silence is usually interrupted by applause from someone who thinks the symphony is over. We try to abolish intervals by our manic insistence on keeping busy, on doing something. And as a result, all we succeed in doing is destroying all hope of tranquillity.

Many Eastern systems have been conspicuously more successful. They have fostered the art of the meaningful pause. They give equal value to object and interval, and by perceiving space as an area of change and expression, they create rhythm. Because intervals are incomplete, they invite participation. They foster a complete experience of things and events in relationship, as distinct from the partial sensation of seeing them in separation.

This seems to be the only way to really understand. You have to learn to immerse yourself in the silences between.

The *djuru* did this.

There is no known sense organ that can give a man underwater the capacity for locating things precisely in the dark, or for responding appropriately to the precursors of a seismic wave. I believe he was able to do these things because he turned his whole body on and tuned in completely to the entire spectrum of information. He listened to the waves and heard not only their news but signals in the silence between them. He measured the intervals and established a beat produced by interference between these waves and others elsewhere. And in this way he put his consciousness in a position to transcend the physical limits of information transfer.

The *djuru* in his oceanic element is part of the pool of all consciousness. He touches the pinnacles of omniscience, omnipresence, and omnipotence. He fulfills, if only momentarily, all man's godliness.

He enters sacred time.

He dances.

Man and His Image

The ocean is indiscrete, forcing connections on her creatures.

In that world of shifting currents, the pull of the moon is as clear to consciousness as the tug of tides on a body.

Water suspends both gravity and disbelief, making it possible for every creeping thing to fly.

Buoyant bodies merge with floating minds.

When I need to restore my integrity, I always take to the sea. Stripping off restrictive clothing and ideology and immersing myself in a medium where space, time, and self seem to merge most easily.

On Nus Tarian it was particularly effective because the water was warm and clear, and I could not succumb to the temptation to cling to equipment in the form of fins, mask, and tanks of air.

It was just me and the sea.

And when I tired of the placid lagoon, I would walk over the hills to Telok Ketjil, where the waves ran right in to the shore.

If the news they carried was local, then their shape would be short and uneasy. But if the fetch was far, they would heave in measured response to the shallows and curl over in long clean lines, breaking where the depth of the water was exactly one third again as great as their height. It was easy to swim out to this nexus point and take advantage of their confusion.

If you launch yourself at the wave front just as it is about to collapse, swim a few strong strokes to match its momentum, and then throw your arms down to rest with hands on the front of thighs so that your whole body forms a taut, slightly convex spar, you can become part of that wave. You share completely in its final moments, shooting in to the shallows with only your head and shoulders protruding from the creaming surf.

At times like that, with the strength and steadiness of the sea working directly on and with me, I could begin to understand the mind of the dolphin. I felt the unity that makes it possible for thought and experience to take place simultaneously. I knew what it was like to be at one with the world.

Between the coast of the northland and the foot of Gunung Iri is an open plain. A wide, flat area which the people call Padang Malas, "the lazy space."

Here, in the southeast trades, the children come to fly kites in the form of moons, birds, and demons, all covered with elaborate designs cut from thin translucent paper. Some of them fix bowlike vibrators to the necks of their kites, and in that season the air hums and buzzes with activity.

Now, in the time of rice, the space was quiet and empty.

On my way back from the surf one morning I walked slowly across the plain, watching the heat haze shimmer just above the surface of the ground.

In a corner, the people had laid out a sprawling pattern of giant clam shells, which were filled with sea water in the dry season and allowed to evaporate to produce salt. Now they too were deserted, flashing bright and white in the sun.

I threaded my way through this strange landscape and into the shade of a grove of *kenari*—huge trees with small leaves and edible nuts which grew only in this one spot on the island.

As my eyes adapted to the sudden leafy gloom, I realized I was not alone there. At the back of the shadowy nave lay a fallen tree, and on the trunk sat Tia with a little girl.

I recognized the child as the daughter of Bebas, a charcoal burner who chose to live out here away from the village. She was about four years old, a very serious child with huge, questioning black eyes.

Tia was talking to her and the child listened solemnly, trying to fit whatever new information she was being given into her burgeoning world view. As children will at that critical age, taking everything adults say or do at face value, and scrutinizing it for meaning.

I couldn't hear their words, but Tia seemed to be having some difficulty making her point. I watched her stop and search the air for inspiration. Then she stood up, and even I, standing way back in the shadows, was included in the conversation.

She began to dance.

Tia started by moving gently round the clearing where they sat, establishing a ground. She flowed out away from this form, including the trunks of the nearest trees in her pattern. She lifted her arms up high and feathered her fingers in an intricate filigree of leaves, relating to the canopy of life and light overhead.

The little girl bounced up and down in happy agreement, and I found myself looking round at the trees with new pleasure.

All Tia had done in her unique, expressive way was to say, "Open your eyes and see. Isn't it lovely?"

It was.

Once she had succeeded in making us conscious of the trees, the form of the dance changed.

She stood in the center of the ground and with a series of emphatic gestures introduced herself into the scene. Where a moment before there had been nothing but the beauty of the grove, now we became aware of Tia in the pattern of the trees. They were, and she was, and as far as we were concerned that was fine too. She looked good there.

Then she did something impossible to describe.

She seemed hardly to move. It wasn't a group of gestures or a fixed pattern of steps—nothing that could be choreographed. But nevertheless, it was real. It had little to do with dance, and yet it was the essence of all great dancing. What it achieved was to convey a feeling, to make a suggestion, and when it was done, we were different. The trees existed, Tia existed, and somehow there was a vital connection between them.

She repeated it again and again with subtle shifts in emphasis—looking at it from other angles, but always saying the same thing. Setting up the trees, putting herself in the picture, creating an elegant notion of the idea of the trees in her mind, and equating this with the reality of the trees around her. Letting us look backwards and forwards between trees around and trees within; allowing us to establish that there was no difference.

Then she did a terrible thing.

She blotted out the image in her mind, and the other trees vanished with it.

We had been seesawing between the two, getting comfortable with the notion of alternatives, and then she abolished them both together.

One moment Tia danced in a grove of shady *kenari*; the

next she was standing alone in the hard, bright light of the sun.

My head reeled, and I blinked and rubbed my eyes until the grove began to grow at the edge of my vision and irised in until it was once again complete.

I feel certain the little girl shared the entire experience with me, but it didn't bother her at all. She leaped to her feet and rushed around touching the trees, laughing gaily, and then stopped in front of Tia.

She stood there big-eyed and earnest. Then she covered her eyes with her hands, taking the world away.

She opened up again and there it was.

On, off; on, off.

She and Tia linked hands and danced together, skipping, the little girl still laughing with the pleasure of understanding, until Tia too started to giggle and the two of them ended up leaning helplessly against the trunk of a tree.

That was the only time I ever saw Tia dance in this way. Relating by means of her dance specifically to someone else. It was a beautiful thing to watch, to see her trying to teach and succeeding in getting the child wonderfully involved. But it was sad too, because it was a measure of her loneliness.

She had always been solitary, but the choice had been hers. Now the pressures of being different, of making people feel uncomfortable, were alienating her from them just when she most needed to communicate, when she had something important to say. In her dancing she usually forgot herself, surrendering totally to the form. The things she said were never aimed at an audience, but addressed exclusively to the relevant divinity. The fact that all those present were inevitably involved was a measure of her success and not her intent. I think she realized that the power of the dance would disintegrate if it were ever to become a spectacle, if through it she sought to influence people rather than spirits.

The dances I experienced on Nus Tarian could never be seen anywhere else. You can't take a dream on tour. Both dance and dream are brought into being by the consciousness of a moment. They can never be repeated or successfully imitated. But you can dance and dream again. You must, if life is to continue.

Dancing is surely the most basic and relevant of all forms of expression. Nothing else can so effectively give outward form to an inner experience. Poetry and music exist in time. Painting and architecture are a part of space. But only the dance lives at once in both space and time. In it the creator and the thing created, the artist and the expression, are one. Each participates completely in the other. There could be no better metaphor for an understanding of the mechanics of the cosmos.

We begin to realize that our universe is in a sense brought into being by the participation of those involved in it. It is a dance, for participation is its organizing principle. This is the important new concept of quantum mechanics. It takes the place in our understanding of the old notion of observation, of watching without getting involved. Quantum theory says it can't be done. That spectators can sit in their rigid row as long as they like, but there will never be a performance unless at least one of them takes part. And conversely, that it needs only one participant, because that one is the essence of all people and the quintessence of the cosmos.

So I wasn't surprised to find Tia holding a class of instruction in the nature of space-time. And when I thought about it, it didn't seem strange that a child should be able to grasp the complex notion that reality is constructed by the mind. It is not a new notion. Parmenides, Bishop Berkeley, James Jeans, and some of our other best and most visionary minds have at one time or another tried to come to terms with it. But it is something self-evident to every child.

I'm not suggesting that Tia or any other child understands the theoretical implications of such a construct. Just that children hold it and know it to be true.

I am certain that Tia had, in addition to a feeling for her role as a participant, some notion of the consequences. As she developed, it became clear that she had an instinctive appreciation of the essence of quantum theory—that wanting something changes the thing you want. She gave up wanting and let herself change. And in this way it was she who actually set the scene for the clash that followed. She sowed the seeds of her own destruction.

Marduk made the first move. He put down the official line in his sermon next Friday at noon.

The text from the Quran was a well-known section in the sura called Al-Nisa that deals with idols.

"Allah will not forgive idolatry. Do not stray from the truth. Only pagans pray to females."

Not once did he mention Tia or the things she did, but he

made it quite clear that to be involved in any way with her was to risk being "cast into hell: a dismal end."

The people were far too kindly to take any overt action against Tia, who may have been disconcerting, but who was, after all, little more than a child.

But Marduk's message had its effect. Rumors about her began to spread.

Tia was seen carrying a white cockerel on the path to Desa Langit, but nobody saw her arrive there with it. The conjecture was that she had taken it to sacrifice at Namata.

This led to the inference that she must be pregnant, and since nobody was known to have been with her, there was speculation about all kinds of demonic possession.

Someone said that someone else had passed her on a path and then found, on turning around, that she had totally disappeared.

If a child cried out in its sleep, it was inevitable that someone would claim to have seen Tia passing by at that very moment.

Tia seldom preened herself in front of mirrors like the other girls, and the gossip suggested that this was because she cast no reflection.

The stories spread rapidly.

At first they were just silly, and nobody took them very seriously; but rumor is an insidious device. It gathers its own momentum and makes stealthy progress towards ends intended by few of those who get it started.

I didn't like the way it was going and began to feel afraid for Tia's safety.

I started a defense of my own, stirring up sympathy for her amongst children in the school, hoping this would spread to their homes and generate a return to reason. But it changed nothing.

I discovered that Tia had taken that cockerel to the family of the charcoal burner, and I told everyone I met about this. But it was too late for me to be of any help at all.

I spoke to Pak Moudhi and Ibu Suri and pleaded with them to intervene.

It would have been a simple matter for either of them to bring Bebas, the charcoal burner, in to testify or to arrange a public demonstration with Tia in front of a mirror.

But neither would take sides.

I became quite angry with the *kepala adat*, who was in a unique position of authority, supported both by the rule of the spirits and by the rule of law, but he merely rebuked me gently.

"Very often," he said, "the conflict is not what it seems."

It seemed appalling to me.

Tia was being persecuted and ostracized in the most cruel way. Nobody came to her anymore for help in healing. Very few people even spoke to her, and she reverted to her childhood pattern of taking long solitary walks on the beach.

She looked tired and unhappy, and it was clear that Marduk had succeeded in his aim of rendering her powerless.

He had achieved his victory with the minimum of personal involvement, and that obviously pleased him.

But then he made a mistake.

No longer seeing her as any kind of threat to his authority, he began publicly to belittle the things she had done, claiming they were the result of simple tricks which anyone could learn.

He called her a fraud and accused her of deceit.

He goaded her into performing again with the Quranic text "Believe in no apostle unless he brings down fire to consume an offering."

And when a week passed and she still hadn't appeared to take up the challenge, he dismissed her altogether.

That Friday, for the first time since his harassment began, there was no direct or even veiled reference to her in his sermon.

But when the gathering in the mosque broke up at the end of *lohor*, Tia was there waiting at the gate, standing alone, very fierce and small.

The people, as if by arrangement, moved to either side of the entrance, forming a living corridor leading from the gate to the mosque itself.

There was a buzz of conversation to begin with, but it soon became unnaturally quiet as everyone watched the door and waited for Marduk to emerge.

Someone must have warned him, because when he did appear he was wearing the white pilgrimage hat of a haji.

Marduk loomed, dark and forbidding, at the top of the stairs with all the authority of orthodoxy wrapped around him like an impenetrable cloak.

Tia stood, small and defiant, well below his level with her bare feet in the sand of the square.

And yet they were evenly matched.

Her very choice of this arena was an act of bravado that gave her an advantage now reflected in her poise.

The tension between them was almost visible.

For the first time in my life I thought I could see the dark line of their confrontation in the air. It hung there like a shifting suggestion of smoke midway between them.

Time stood still as the conflict raged. Unseen forces clashed in the air. The smoky barrier fluttered, shifted, settled again, and then almost audibly shattered into wisps of shade that hurtled over Marduk and away.

An expression of incomprehension swept over his face, swiftly followed by a moment of realization which was equally quickly replaced by fear.

He had been routed again.

Everyone there knew that something had been resolved, and it was clear which way the decision had gone.

All eyes were turned on Marduk, who was swaying a little on his feet, but then they were drawn irresistibly past and above and beyond him to where a tongue of flame leaped out from the minaret of the mosque.

Fire!

Those nearest to the well went into action.

The bucket was rushed head-high over the crowd, then up the ladder, and after three or four more trips, the blaze was quenched before it could do any great damage. It seemed almost to lose interest and flicker out of its own accord.

And when it was gone, and we stood looking at the black smoke stain on the sheets of white metal around the dome, we realized that Tia had vanished with it.

But she had met the challenge, and whether or not she had had anything to do with it, fire had indeed been "brought down."

When I first became interested in unusual events, I went with several other scientists to visit a house in South Africa that was plagued by more than its fair share of domestic problems. Furniture moved of its own accord; crockery would hang impossibly suspended in midair until it smashed to the floor; stones appeared out of nowhere and fell from the ceiling. The evening of our visit was comparatively quiet—just a few rapping sounds that seemed to come from within the fabric of the walls—but it built up to a grand finale. As we sat round the dining-room table discussing the phenomena with the family, an embroidered lace mat in the center began to smolder. Someone doused it with a glass of water. Then the full-length curtains covering a picture window leading out into the garden burst suddenly and completely into flame as though they had been primed with petroleum.

Poltergeists are common. Every police force in the world must have at least one in its files. And everywhere they follow much the same kind of pattern. Disturbances are usually short-lived and, unlike hauntings, seem to be centered not so much on a place as around a particular individual. Most often this person is an adolescent; a distribution curve of those involved falls mainly between the ages of ten and twenty, with a majority being female. In a high proportion of cases there is obvious nervous tension in the individual or in the family situation. And in a significant number there are overt signs of psychoneurosis manifested as hysteria, such as blindness or paralysis. In the South African case the focus of the events was a thirteen-year-old spastic girl; and after three weeks of intense activity, everything stopped abruptly on the precise date of her first menstruation.

Several researchers have now completed detailed psychological profiles of individuals who are either the agents or the targets of poltergeist activities, and there is a consistent pattern. Most have trouble with verbal expression. Often this is coupled with hostility which is suppressed from consciousness. And there are feelings of frustration produced by an inability to express hostility overtly. These findings have been used as the grounds for a theory which describes all the happenings as examples of displaced aggression. It suggests that what takes place is a sort of nonverbal communication. An acting out of repressed hostility by unknown energetic means.

This puts poltergeists into the same category as psychokinesis, turning those special people who seem to be able to produce changes in matter by purely mental means into conscious poltergeists. Which makes sense, but brings us no closer to a real understanding of either phenomenon.

The most valuable insight into this problem area lies in the investigation of those who were once unconscious poltergeist agents and who have now become practicing conscious psychokineticists. Matthew Manning of Cambridge in England is one of these. He graduated from moving furniture and noises in the night to automatic drawing, telepathy, metal bending, and most recently to healing. His gifts as a schoolboy made him an object of curiosity, something of interest, but not someone to get too close to lest you catch his affliction. It is hardly surprising, therefore, that Matthew, now twenty-two, is somewhat reserved, but he can in no way be described as psychotic or neurotic. In my contact with him, I have found him to be very well balanced, completely composed, and intensely interested in the difficult problem of finding scientific explanations for the things he does so easily.

Classical psychoanalytic theory recognizes two distinct groups of function in a personality. On one side are automatic abilities which enable us to move around and perceive and to think about things; on the other are learned patterns, such as how we relate to other people or defend ourselves from them. The first type are all free of conflict and can have nothing to do with poltergeistery. The second could be involved, but as the phenomena seem to be entirely involuntary, they can be seen as symptoms of a defense pattern only as long as the conflict that caused them remains unconscious. The mysterious happenings are rather like fever symptoms in an illness; they are part of the cure and have nothing directly to do with the disease. When the cure is complete, when the conflict is resolved, they ought to disappear. In fact, very few poltergeists have a life span of more than a few weeks.

Manning, of course, is different. His talents continue to develop and he remains eminently sane. Joel Whiton, a Toronto physician involved in psychic research, suggests that phenomena may be able to persist for a longer time if their activity becomes independent—rather like a nervous tic which sometimes continues after the anxiety that produced it has been resolved. Both tic and talent can move into the area of voluntary conscious control.

Most adults who do unusual things consciously are nevertheless sufficiently disturbed by them to reserve at least one last line of defense. They insist that the phenomena are controlled by spirit guides, electromagnetism, or extraterrestrial beings. They project the blame onto God, science, or UFOs. But the probability is that each and every one of us has complete control of all the necessary equipment.

Children have easiest access to it. In the first few years of life, everything has a magical quality. Before minds ossify into the channels prescribed by the current educational formula, all events are shrouded in mystery. They take place in a world where anything is possible. Objects appear and disappear, the sun rises and sets, people come and go. As a child's mind moves to take all these things into account, it begins to make connections and to draw inferences without having access to all the facts. This leads to conclusions that to us seem bizarre and totally delusional. Holding your breath for a long time is a good way to make the sun stay behind a cloud. Counting very quickly up to twenty while you stand on one leg with your eyes closed is how to make a wish come true. Thinking about a tire blowout is enough to cause the thing actually to happen. Isn't it?

Can you really be certain that there is no causal connection? Do you know beyond doubt that your thoughts have no influence over your environment? No modern physicist shares your certitude. The most advanced cosmologies all include consciousness as an active participating factor. And the new equations are very much like the old beliefs of children everywhere. Undogmatic young minds are much concerned with magic, and as a result they arrive at descriptions of reality that to us seem faulty, but in the final analysis prove to be far more meaningful than those we contrive by the elaborate exercise of logic and contingent mathematics. It seems that merely by admitting the possibility of unlikely events, you increase the probability of their occurence. And the cosmos is filled with unlikely happenings.

In Toronto a group of people started an experiment in which they attempted to experience a collective hallucination. They tried to conjure up a ghost. Not the specter of a long-dead individual, but the vision of a completely fictitious seventeenth-century nobleman. They called him Philip and compiled a detailed imaginary biography for him beforehand so that his manifestation, if it should take place, could not be confused with that of a real spirit. For two years they struggled, but nothing happened until a session when several members of the group were involved in some childlike horseplay. Then the table round which they were seated began to rock. They have still not seen Philip, but today, by consciously attempting to behave like children, by singing silly songs and regressing to the point where their communal thinking once again takes on magical qualities, they can produce psychokinetic phenomena at will. While I sat with the Philip group one evening they became involved in a long and splendidly bawdy conversation with their imaginary ghost, who ended the session by lifting a very heavy table until all four legs were off the ground and pursuing the photographer from an American magazine round the room with it until it had him pinned to a wall.

No single person in that group has conscious control over

what will happen, and not one of them is indispensable. All they need is a quorum. It is psychokinesis by committee, and by communal agreement that such things are possible. The conscious acceptance of such an agreement is simplified by invention of the projection they call Philip, and facilitated by suspension of normal rules and responsibilities in their deliberately childlike approach. But what they have shown is that any group of people, ordinary folk without a single psychic pretension among them, can produce, on demand and at will, well-developed paranormal phenomena. Anyone can get round the rules of traditional science simply by pretending they don't exist.

John Taylor, the professor of mathematics at Kings College in London, has been making heroic attempts to get the framework of classical physics to bend far enough to accommodate psychokinetic phenomena. He began working with Uri Geller and went on to perform an elegant series of experiments with children who, having seen the Israeli psychic perform on television, started to repeat his mental metal-bending feats for themselves. In the past three years this group have quite independently come up with a number of variations of their own invention, and Taylor has followed them every step of the way, recording and analyzing, setting up experiments to eliminate the possibility of fraud and to test possible theories.

Taylor dismisses radioactive, nuclear, or gravitational forces as candidates because none of them could be wielded by a human body with sufficient force to bend a paper clip, let alone a stainless-steel spoon. That leaves him with only one of the four natural forces recognized by science—electromagnetism. He pins all his faith on this, suggesting that humans are capable of producing and emitting an electromagnetic "intentionality field" which interacts with other matter. And after examining several possible carrier mechanisms such as low-frequency oscillations working on existing dislocations in metal objects, he concludes that the phenomena will be completely understood only when we can build an electrochemical machine to duplicate their effect.

I admire John Taylor's persistence, but I fear he is destined for disappointment. Any totally materialistic interpretation of the universe cannot account for even the best-known properties of the brain such as memory, let alone those effects which have their basis in consciousness. And I fear, too, that many of the experiments now being done in Europe and North America on Geller, Manning, and others with well-developed talents will prove to be a waste of time. It is interesting to know that someone produces a special set of brain-wave functions while bending a key, but I don't believe it means any more than the observation that his hands perspire while he is thinking about a special friend. The measurements are purely symptomatic and tell us absolutely nothing about the key, the girl, or the relationship of either to that mind which seems to be at least in part responsible for their existence. Looking for physical explanations of mind is like attacking a piano with a sledgehammer to get at the concerto imprisoned inside. It is a lunatic endeavor.

The basic fallacy is that there must necessarily be some form of energy flow involved in all transactions. This may be totally untrue. I feel more comfortable with the kind of philosophical idealism that dispenses altogether with the idea of matter. Although this could be an equally extreme position, it seems likely to prove a more fruitful starting point for investigation of man—and the images he has of himself and of the world around him.

In 1714 the German mathematician Leibniz proposed the existence of nonspatial, indestructible, indivisible entities he called monads. He saw them as wholly psychic in nature—

made up entirely of the qualities of mind. They were dismissed at the time as hypothetical nonsense, but today they no longer look quite so ridiculous. For his dominant monad, the one in ultimate control, read collective consciousness or universal mind, and situate it somewhere beyond the bounds of space-time in superspace. On the next level of this cosmic hierarchy, in normal space-time, comes the matter-creating monad we call consciousness or mind. Put this in charge of unfolding physical systems with their infinite numbers of states, make it amenable to some form of democracy or consensus that governs lawful and orderly operation—and you have the makings of a workable system.

The attractive feature of such a model is that it allows anything to happen. If Bohm is right about matter's appearing to move through space by constantly being destroyed and re-created, then it should be no more difficult for the mind monad to bend a spoon than it is for it to bend a finger. If you can think of a bent spoon, you can have a bent spoon. If all forms of matter are merely thoughts in the mind monad, then their positions and properties are readily interchangeable. Materialization, dematerialization, teleportation, and levitation become simple matters of a change of mind. If consciousness can drop at will out of normal space-time into superspace, where there is no such thing as time and thought travels faster than light, then instant thought transference, precognition, retrocognition, and clairvoyance are all easy. And if consciousness can return to space-time at any location, past, present, or future, and experience these locations, then we have time travel, space travel, and travel out of the body. With such free movement of consciousness, it is of course possible to know every detail of the life of everyone who ever lived, and that takes care of reincarnation.

So it goes. It is all very easy when you can just juggle

around with ideas like this; anyone can play that kind of academic game. But the wonderful thing about this is that it is strongly supported by much recent scientific theory.

John Wheeler's concept of superspace involves a quantum-mechanical scattering of an indefinite number of coexisting universes all interconnected by "wormholes" which carry signals like nerve cells feeding a great cosmic brain. He suggests that the entire universe may consist of only one electron which is scattered in time to perform all particle functions everywhere.

Harris Walker sees space as inhabited by an unlimited number of interconnected conscious entities responsible for the detailed workings of the universe, answerable for each event involving every individual particle. Consciousness, he says, is everywhere.

Jack Sarfatti believes that consciousness distorts space and time by knocking black holes in the biogravitational field that organizes matter. He thinks that gravity may also turn out to be the carrier that brings consciousness into the system from beyond space-time.

Fred Wolf suggests that order, in the shape of the reality we know best, is introduced by the fact that the path of history takes the line of least action between two events. It creates the least cosmic disturbance.

But he goes on to say that every time we make a measurement, every time we get involved, we stop the world, and this changes it in a way that puts the path of least action in another place. Existence produces awareness, which changes existence, and so on.

These are some of our top theoretical physicists struggling to come to terms with what we now know about the world. Their ideas are bound to change and grow as consciousness grows. Nothing is certain except that there is no going back to the easy optimism of the Age of Reason. The cosmos is an unreasonable state of affairs that seems to owe more to mood than to method. It dances to music inaudible to individual ears, but it is just possible to pick up the rhythm if you concentrate on being rather than doing. If you get deeply involved, as children do.

Tia had the advantage of having been raised in several different disciplines, all of which acknowledged the existence of spirit as a determining factor. She was able to cope with the discrepancies in their descriptions of reality by accepting them all and making no value judgments about them. In this she was encouraged by the fact that Islam on Nus Tarian was very flexible, blending with traditional animistic and pantheistic beliefs wherever it had to. So her world view was one predisposed to the acceptance of almost anything. Her isolation as a child, like the withdrawal of Manning at the same age, led to social conflicts, which in her case did not need to be acted out in poltergeistery because at that very time she learned to express herself in dance. But later, partly as a result of her trigger experience with the whale, her conflicts were resolved and the talents came under conscious control. She began to choose her realities. A "conscious poltergeist" of that kind would have very little difficulty in starting a remote fire. Matter in flame is simply that matter with its molecules accelerated to the point where it catches fire.

I am certain that the mosque incident came under her full conscious control. There is no doubt she wanted a fire, because that was what Marduk had asked for. But her earlier feats and the phenomena produced by most psychics seem to be under only limited control. Neither Uri Geller nor Matthew Manning is ever quite certain what will happen when they "turn their power on."

If space-time is a construct of our mind, then it seems that superspace may be the product of a cosmic mind. We return to the notion of an intelligent earth nourished in its turn by an intelligent system of energy. The collapse of a system in normal space-time into an appropriate state is subject to rules of orderliness that predicate the selection of certain states rather than others. Consciousness chooses the path of least action and disturbance. It is itself the product of a self-organizing field in space-time and enjoys a certain amount of autonomy there, but it also has roots that go deeper, into the realms of superspace. It has connections with superconsciousness or the cosmic mind.

I suggest that the special people, the ones who break the rules, who are deflected from the path of least action into improbable areas outside space-time, are in closer contact with that cosmic intellect than the rest of us. They are perhaps less completely unfolded. It is not a matter of their having superconsciousness, but rather of their just happening to be on one of the paths of least action between two events, or between space and superspace.

So they do unusual things. Sometimes these seem to be completely meaningless. There is no message in or practical function for a bent spoon. Yet Geller and all those influenced by him keep on giving the same demonstration. There have been a few nice variations, like the ten-year-old British boy who produces attractive twisted metal sculptures with his mind, or the Japanese children who turn tennis balls inside out. But on the whole there is very little imagination or direction manifest in the occurrences; they tend to focus on objects that come readily to hand and to deal with these in the accepted way. The saucer shape of so many UFOs and the humpedness of the Loch Ness Monster are comparable conventions.

Perhaps all these things should be regarded as tics produced by some conflict in the cosmic mind. Maybe the talent for seeing or doing things is an unconscious manifestation of a cosmic want or need. The connections between space and superspace seem to be governed by a type of orderliness that normally functions well, but perhaps some of these links become strained and, in order to relieve tensions which we cannot yet even begin to imagine, tiny changes in position have to be made. This area of the paranormal would then be one of regulation, a kind of balance zone where minor adjustments can take place. It may be that some such alterations require the assistance of consciousness, in which case the events act as triggers that get minds actively involved in what is going on. By taking notice of the phenomena, by thinking about them, admitting they exist, and looking for explanations, we may be doing all that is necessary to redress the balance and iron out ambiguity.

But not all psychokinetic events are meaningless. Some show evidence of a kind of whimsy, and a few are very funny. Poltergeists sometimes begin to look like practical jokers. There was one in the United States that scribbled an interminable shaggy-dog story on the walls of an isolated farmhouse. And in the Philippines I watched a healer take a large bird's nest, complete with feathers and broken shells, from the navel of a patient who complained of "fluttering in the stomach." Where touches of humor are present, I suspect that human consciousness is probably involved to a greater extent, imposing its own cultural patterns on the events.

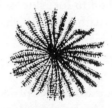

And whenever the phenomena are totally appropriate and meaningful, as in a full healing situation, I think we can expect to find close cooperation between cosmic needs and human wants. This does not mean that Tia sat by the bride's side thinking, What can I do that will impress her most powerfully? Tia had access to power and to all the infinite number of possible states, and she was guided to the right one in a totally unconscious way. She wanted her friend to be well, and her want, superimposed on the power structure, created a new and appropriate path of least action. Everything in her work fell naturally into place because she was in tune with the situation. She did the right thing because it also happened to be the beautiful thing. It fitted.

The fire in the mosque was appropriate, but hardly beautiful. It was a terrifying demonstration and owed more to Tia's overriding personality than to any cosmic intellect.

The results were dramatic.

There was no longer the possibility that Pak Moudhi or anyone else could defend her. Tia had finally gone too far, and the people felt it was dangerous to have her around. There was talk of prayer and exorcism, of the revival of an ancient technique of whipping evil out, and of sending her to Djakarta. But nothing could be done without the consent of Abu, who was her guardian.

Abu was a very pious and orthodox Muslim, and he was shocked by the desecration of the mosque. He had taken no part in the celebration of Tia's early powers because the idea of healing in that way made him feel uncomfortable. But now he refused to come out against her.

The people respected him, and so for several days there was an impasse. But finally the pressure became so great that Abu advised Tia to leave the village.

She fled one night to Desa Langit, where, rumor had it, Pak Moudhi found her a place to stay. And so for several weeks she simply disappeared from sight, and the campaign against her gradually subsided until it no longer seemed quite so important.

Harvest time was near and the people's thoughts and energies turned to the matter of rice.

About a month after the last water is drained from the land, the rice is ready to harvest. Turning the growing *padi* into the raw husked *beras* is an awesome undertaking, filled with risk and elaborately guarded by ritual.

All living things are seen to have *segamat*, spirit, but rice alone is said to have a soul. *Djiwa*, the soul, lives happily in the fields where the rice grows, but has to be enticed to stay with the crop after harvesting. So work always begins in the most remote sawah, and cutting the grain stalks just below the ear with sharp little knives, the entire community moves like a line of beaters, driving the rice soul ahead of them from field to field. Where a path or any other space lies between one sawah and the next, the people help *djiwa* across by building a solid bridge of rice bundles. In this way an unbroken chain of connection is created leading from the distant fields all the way in to the village.

When the work ended one day at dusk in the last and nearest patch of *padi*, Pak Moudhi arrived in costume carrying an old lantern which he held aloft while he told *djiwa* how great was the people's respect and how lavish the welcome prepared in the special thatched barns built on stilts in the village. He explained in detail how to get there, taking great care to indicate points where there were crossroads and it was possible to make a mistake. At each of these places, a small shrine was built a little way down the path on the village side of the junction to lead the soul on in the right direction.

On the following morning, the buffalo came out with sleds and hauled all the neatly tied bundles of grain into the safety and shelter of Kota Rendah.

The weather continued fine, and threshing began almost immediately. This was done by the women, who laid rice bundles on the ground and pounded them with round-ended wooden poles to free the heads. The stalks were raked away, leaving chaff to be spread out on flat circular baskets. Then, when the wind was just right, strong enough to blow away only the husks, they sat with these baskets on their laps and coaxed the seeds into final freedom with a lovely drifting song in the old tongue that told again of Hainuwele and her gifts to the world.

Finally, the grain was stored in huge bins in the barns and the soul was thought to be reasonably secure; but rice still had to be treated with proper respect. The correct procedure when going to a store is to choose an auspicious moment, the late afternoon is best, and first make your apologies to *djiwa*.

"Forgive this intrusion, but we need some more rice. You won't be hurt if we take a little?"

Then measure out the required portion, taking great care to do so gently. And before leaving, add a little more oil and water to the two bowls placed in every barn so that the soul may wash and comb her hair, because *djiwa* is unquestionably female.

This elaborate concern for a basic food crop is not just a quaint local custom. It is shared by all people close to the land in a common belief that every time you cut a blade of grass, you shake the universe. Modern physics tends to agree. Our universe seems to be one of unbroken wholeness in which every part is directly connected to every other part. The latest scientific name for the soul is "hidden variable," but whatever you call it, it seems to be firmly rooted in consciousness. And it would appear to be prudent to make a conscious attempt to regulate as far as possible the effects on the universe of cutting a good many blades of grass all at once. The next crop and your survival may depend on it. If you are obliged to shoot an arrow into the air, it makes sense to ensure that it is properly flighted so that you have some chance of predicting where it will fall. You hope for the line of least action, the appropriate path. Everything, as usual, revolves around a question of balance and responsibility. Of proper regard for the world and your place in it.

Even while reaping was still in progress, it was obvious that this had been an exceptional year for Nus Tarian. There would certainly be a rice surplus for trade with the Bugis and neighboring islands.

In the fields and on the threshing floor the word "Maro" began to be mentioned, at first hesitantly for fear of provoking some last-minute disaster, but towards the end quite openly.

So it came as no surprise to anyone when, on the night the last seed went into store, Pak Moudhi announced it would be fitting to offer a thanksgiving feast to the rice spirit, starting on the day before the next full moon.

It had been nine years since the last such celebration, and to most of the children "Maro" was no more than a word.

But it was a magic word.

Preparations began immediately, with each of the nine clans playing its traditional role.

The buffalo people prepared the sacred place of the Nine Dance Grounds, cutting, cleaning, sweeping, and stamping fresh droppings and blood into the earth to produce a smooth, hard floor for the dancers.

The fish clan, that of Pak Moudhi himself, was responsible

for recruiting and training the dancers and ensuring that all were familiar with the patterns and forms of *adat*.

The families of the butterfly made costumes.

The deer people were the music makers, and they could be heard rehearsing late into the night in a shed built expressly for this purpose a short way down the beach on the lagoon.

Food for the feast was prepared by the bird clan with contributions from everyone else.

Rice and palm wine were fermented by the clam people, and for once, the imam pretended not to notice.

The crab clan made coconut-oil lamps to form a glowing avenue out from the village and to encircle the dance ground itself.

The crocodile family, who are traditional rainmakers, were required to provide fine weather for the occasion. A formidable task even now at the end of the rainy season.

And to the turtle clan fell the honor of composing an entirely new set of songs on the traditional themes of thanksgiving.

For two weeks all other activities on the island came to a halt. School was dismissed, trading and farming ground to a standstill, and only those fishermen who belonged to the bird clan continued to exercise their usual skills. Everyone talked of, sang to, worked for, or dreamed about nothing but the Maro.

Having no traditional function of my own, I simply wandered from family to family, chatting, looking and listening.

Conversation in the working groups was wonderful. There were jokes and riddles, new poems and old stories. The air was constantly filled with laughter and repartee in which even the most staid and conservative took part. The children sat on the edges open-mouthed with astonishment at this unsuspected aspect of their parents.

I gloried in it all, learning more about the people in those few days than I had in months gone by.

I enjoyed most of all reminiscence about the old days and other Maro celebrations, but as I listened I began to detect a note of concern about this one.

In other, more heroic times, it was said, the Maro lasted for nine nights and took place on nine entirely separate dance grounds; but as long as anyone could remember the ceremony on Nus Tarian had been telescoped into one night of dancing in one place. This nevertheless began as the sun went down and didn't stop again until the dawn.

I gathered that of the nine traditional forms, all were choral dances except the last, the dance of Hainuwele herself, dedicated directly to the rice soul, which had to be performed solo by a young girl. And that ever since she had turned eight and gone to study with Ibu Suri, everyone had known that when the time for the next Maro came, they would have in Tia a dancer worthy of the solo role.

But now?

I went up to Desa Langit to watch the dancers in rehearsal and found Pak Moudhi putting them through their paces.

Ibu Suri belonged to the butterfly clan and should have been down in Kota Rendah sewing costumes, but she had no patience with such finicky things and everyone was glad to regard her as an honorary fish.

She was leading a young girl through an intricate form, and the glade in which they practiced was rich with the rhythm of her calls. The girl was one of the three who had danced for me and my crewmen of the *Little Flower* on the day we arrived. She was very good, but she wasn't Tia, and I could see it was breaking the old lady's heart.

There was no sign of Tia in the upper village.

Nobody seemed to know anything of her whereabouts, and

I knew better than to ask Pak Moudhi any direct questions about her.

It was as if she had ceased to exist.

There was tacit agreement amongst the people not to mention her at all, but just beneath all talk of the Maro was the wistful thought "Wouldn't it be nice if . . ."

At last the day came.

Everyone was up before the sun, busily involved in final preparations, and at noon the feast began.

Pak Suran and his clan had built tables in a circle out in the coconut plantation and decorated them with palm fronds and plate after plate of breadfruit, fried banana, shark chutney, boiled papaya, grilled octopus, rock lobster, clam soup, steamed fish, raw fish, baked fish, fish curry, beef curry, carameled prawns, eggs in sour sauce, salads, satis, relishes, spices, cakes, fruits, and sweetmeats. In the center of the circle, on a special fireplace, stood three huge caldrons turning out an avalanche of *nasi*, boiled rice—staple and preferred food, and the reason for the feast.

All afternoon we ate and drank, we swam and played. There were fights between champion cocks with wicked spurs of polished steel wired to their feet. Each brief, bloody battle in a small sandy square was preceded by an uproar of verbal transactions, too fast for me to follow but apparently comprehensible to all taking part.

I preferred the fighting tops—huge polished hardwood disks that were cracked down into a playing circle by rival teams, mainly of the older men. And the long-spinning tops, slim, streamlined, inlaid with bone and metal for balance, scooped up off the ground and set under special canopied bamboo stands where they could "sleep" more easily in the shade. The winner kept humming there for more than an hour before it fell.

At sunset, the ceremony began.

We all assembled on the beach, and as the sun went down Pak Moudhi took a handful of rice and threw it out over the sea, making an offering to Great Turtle, who had raised the island from the ocean floor and put it into the air where wind and rain make rice and life come true.

Then the lamps were lit and we went in silent procession back through the village, out along the flare path to the place of the Nine Dance Grounds. The musicians took their places, and Pak Moudhi stood in the center with his hands raised for silence.

He said, "This is our year."

And the people replied, "Give us our season."

"This is our home."

"Give us our children."

"This is our body."

"Give us our reason."

The *kepala adat* lifted both arms in a wide dramatic gesture and added very simply, "So, we dance."

For a long time nothing happened.

Then I trembled at a touch in the center of my being. There was nothing yet that could be seen or heard, but something had begun.

Very slowly I became conscious of the echo of a rhythm, of the pulse of something distant but part of me.

Part of all of us, for everywhere around me people were taking up the beat. The blink of her eye, the movement of his head, there the lift of a shoulder or the tremble of a knee, here a tightening in my gut. We were being carried along in synchrony by the same deep invisible current.

Then we heard it, the very cadence of being.

Not a cosmic hiss or the smooth, round sound of consciousness, but a vibrant discord of sheer vitality, of life busy living.

As the static quivered around us, the dancers came into view. Two long lines, women in one and men in the other, winding onto the arena, dressed in brief woven costumes, and strapped to the ankles of every participant, pleated boxes of dry palm leaf filled with small stones that rattled so that each step was punctuated by a shatter of sound.

This was the first choral dance, the restless, stirring *pedoa* with which every Maro began.

The dancers formed a circle with arms linked. Pak Moudhi moved into the center and started a lilting chant, most of it on one high note. Two male dancers broke away, joining him to set the pace, and the ring began to move anticlockwise, rocking and stamping with every beat.

It started slowly, feet pounding and rattling in a heavy measure, but inexorably it picked up speed until the *kepala adat*'s voice was a single stream of sound. The circle spun and pounded with an insistent, almost feverish rhythm, goading the world into matching its pace.

We throbbed with it, happily and desperately, moved to total participation, rising to an incredible climax when all the feet and all the voices hit the some loud sound simultaneously, and then suddenly stopped.

For a moment there was absolute silence, and then the women took up their shimmering cry of praise.

I have heard it often in Africa, given to Masai or Zulu warriors-in-arms. I have been in the Wadi Rum when the Bedouin women in the hills salute the Arab Legion passing through. And still it moves me as no other sound ever can. A liquid, trembling, high-pitched resonance that anthropologists call ululating. But that flat, clinical Western word says nothing about the fervor in the cry that can put fire into the blood even of a dead man.

With the second dance form the musicians came into their own, and melodies both played and sung began to take their part in the celebration, creating connections between the dance themes and the magic purpose of every movement.

Much of what happened for the rest of the night exists in my mind only as a blur of sound and color. Serpentine forms and meanders, place changing and crossing rounds, chain dances, return dances, dances with kris and stave, leaping, gliding, intricate filigrees of tone, great curves of melody and texture.

It is impossible to recall it all in detail, but one sensation is absolutely clear. That everything was leading in a definite direction, building up to the final form on the ninth ground in which Hainuwele would live again in homage to the soul of rice, a gift she gave to men.

In the last hour of the night, clouds began to build and we were deprived of the moon.

The crocodile family deployed its forces to hold rain in abeyance until after the dancing ended at dawn. It seemed to succeed, because the approaching storm banked up over Gunung Api like a wave in suspension, leaving us in sultry stillness at its foot.

Tension mounted.

When the eighth form ended, the ground was left empty.

Once again we waited, primed this time for the sound.

It started in the distance, that solid rattling stamp, accompanied now by voices chanting in unison.

The lines came into sight and separated at the edge of the ground, the women going straight into a huddle in the middle and the men moving out in a wide arc that circled the entire area and, just before it intersected with itself, cut into the center and began to curl down in a smooth descending spiral.

Tighter and tighter it wound, seeming to vanish into a black hole as people piled up in the middle.

Then, just when it seemed impossible to squeeze any more

into the eye of this human storm, the drums and gongs clashed like thunder and all movement stopped.

Slowly, very slowly, in absolute silence, like a time-lapse sequence of a flower blooming, the people peeled off to reveal, standing there alone in a costume of green and a mask of young palm leaves, the tiny figure of a girl with her hands crossed over her breast.

Frond of the Coco Palm—Hainuwele!

The people held their breath, because what she had to do now was very difficult and very important.

This was the homage to rice and the access to power. The island's continued survival could depend on how well she expressed herself in the traditional Maro form.

She was speaking for all, talking directly to the forces that controlled the cosmos, asking for power, dancing to maintain life itself.

Energy streamed out from the community, willing the child to do well.

The musicians began a soft, yielding melody line, the sound of palm fronds deferring to the wind. It wafted over the girl like a gentle breeze, tugging at her hands until they fluttered in response. Her arms became fronds, bowing gracefully to pressure, bouncing back into place.

The music pushed her a little harder, clamoring for complete submission. She ignored the challenge and the demands became imperious, insisting on capitulation, lashing at her with wild gusts of sound.

She turned slowly away from the blast, apparently on the point of collapse, and then—whirled around and, with a leap and three masterful movements, brought the elements under her total subjugation and control.

The transformation was beautifully done, and everyone breathed easily again.

It was going to be all right.

Now the music followed Hainuwele, and swelling to join it from every throat came a dark-colored humming sound, filling everything with a reverberation that drew us on together as she led the way into the unknown.

After a while she paused and with a wave indicated we should wait while she reconnoitered alone.

The path to power was obviously strewn with difficulties. She drew our attention to these with a few deft flicks of her wrist. Then we watched her begin to negotiate them alone.

This was another testing moment, the one section of the traditional form where improvisation was allowed; but having seen her acquit herself so well in the opening responses, nobody was worried anymore about the new young dancer's letting her people down.

She seemed to be flying very high, free from the restraints of reality.

She began to sketch a scenario for us, using the established language of gesture in which symbols for almost any eventuality are prescribed in the twenty-four movements of the head, four attitudes of the neck, six shapes of the eyebrows, twenty-four expressions of the eyes, and fifty-seven positions of the hands.

Because of the leaf mask in the Maro, the dancer is limited mainly to hand signs and is not expected to attempt any very complex portrayals; but Hainuwele on this night knew no bounds. With an angular twist of the arm she summoned up self-satisfaction and then as quickly dispelled it. With a fleeting finger touch she caricatured greed and sent it away unfulfilled. She revealed jealousy with a flash of her open hands, letting us feel the full force of its corrosion, and then abolished it.

The people began to stir.

She ran through a lightning series of movements that produced all the frightening consequences of hate, cruelty, and intolerance and allowed us to feel their suffering. And at the head of this catalogue of dangers on the road, she established the greatest risk of all attending any searcher after truth—the paramount sin of indifference.

And she let it hang there.

Now the crowd was crackling with attention. The dancer, this spirit of Hainuwele, had started in the conventional way, but then she had changed patterns and not once used any of the customary combinations of gesture.

She had broken every single rule of the dance. And yet, with a series of single strokes she had been able to reveal the ultimate significance of all natural phenomena. She had managed to divest gods, humans, and life of their chance reality and transport them into a dream world where the essence of things, instead of being blurred by our awkward vision, flashed out with the utmost clarity. She had transcended the ritual of formal technique and made the dance a rapturous expression of her own very personal religion.

There was only one person who could possibly do that.

The people all turned to look at each other, and in that moment we knew beyond doubt that this was no novice dancer.

This was Tia.

She knew that we knew, and she simply stood there waiting for a decision to be made.

Nobody moved until Pak Moudhi signaled to the musicians to start the next sequence.

They began, and the people almost sighed with relief. They sensed that what Tia was doing here was in their interest, and they weren't anxious to break the continuity of the Maro by introducing personal animosities. The kepala adat had made the right decision.

The male dancers began building their dynamic ninefold

spiral around the stationary figure in the center, and as is the way in the Maro, Hainuwele handed out betel to them as they passed her. When all had received the gift, they formed a semicircle behind her and she stepped forward to receive the people's gift to her.

It is customary to collect the very first bundle of *padi* and bind it tightly round with pure white silk for this occasion. At the very edge of the dance ground, Pak Moudhi stood with this offering on a tray, waiting to present it to her before she went on to dance the final form which would bring power and protection down on the island's future endeavors.

She moved gracefully forward to stand in front of the *kepala adat*.

Then, just as she was about to take the first fruits of the harvest from his hand, a figure in black stepped in between them and dashed the gift to the ground.

It was Marduk. So tight with a wild black tension that it seemed if he moved again he must shatter. He stood there taut and terrible, with basilisk eyes that were capable of splitting rocks, burning grass, and making birds fall dead at his feet.

Tia stripped off her palm-frond mask and looked directly up at him. The authority of Hainuwele slipped from her and she was once more a child, young and afraid, but resolved on a course of action that might have been right, but promised to be painful.

Marduk saw something there that disconcerted him. It may have been his own reflection. A look almost of admiration touched his face, and for a moment these two understood each other.

At any other time this contact could have nourished the small reluctance each felt for pursuing this conflict to its inevitable end. But it was too late now.

237 • MAN AND HIS IMAGE

Again they clashed. And we knew that this was the final round, that the struggle must be pushed to a conclusion.

It was a duel of giants.

Neither moved a muscle, but the battle was fierce. Skirmish and strain, disengage and regroup, attack again and again.

It was merciless, and it went on until even we could see that neither was going to give way. The smoke was not going to be blown over either head this time. It would have to be blasted away.

It was Marduk who finally broke the deadlock, and it seemed almost as though she let him do it, although she could never have expected anything so terrible.

Marduk lifted his right hand deliberately up to head level as though he would strike her, but then he turned it on himself.

He formed a claw, and pushing his index finger in at the inside corner of his right eye, he levered the eyeball out until it was straining at the muscles that held it in the socket.

Then, with an agonized jerk, he ripped it entirely out, tearing the stalk apart in a spray of blood and tissue.

He held the eye at arm's length above his head, let his breath out in a gasp of pain and achievement, and then offered it to Tia.

The gesture he used was in one movement a summary and an explanation of everything that had happened on Nus Tarian.

It was not a brutal *coup de grâce*, made in desperation and anger to end a conflict that could be resolved in no other way. It was not a psychotic piece of self-mutilation or the futile act of a cornered and badly injured animal that turns to bite itself.

He held out his hand with the bloody offering in it as a real alternative to the gift of first fruit.

It was a proud gesture, a magnificent and defiant one, fully conscious of the fact that it was conclusive, but extending with it a measure of esteem and approval for what she represented.

He was telling her and us that he acknowledged the power and beauty of her way, but that there was a strength in his way too, a raw and very human energy that could not be denied.

By ripping out his right eye, he was sacrificing part of himself.

It was an appalling thing to do; but essentially it was an act of balance, and it required reciprocation.

Tia took the offering in her cupped hands and carried it unsteadily back to the center of the ground. There she emptied the remains of the betel on the ground and, placing the eye in the carved casket, held this up in the traditional gesture of Hainuwele dedicating the people's gift to the spirits.

There had never been one so potent.

Then she placed the box on the ground, and as the musicians began the rippling introduction to the power form, the last great act of the Maro, she turned slowly round to begin the dance.

Tia lifted her arms in the familar stance that always preceded one of her flowing movements—and fell over her feet.

The music faltered and then picked up as she rose to start again, but when she didn't move, it faded away and died.

A hush fell over the dance ground and we waited and watched, willing her to go on.

She wrestled desperately with the inertia, but it was no use. She couldn't do it. The sacrifice had been made.

Tia could no longer dance.

She fell to her knees sobbing.

Pak Moudhi, torn by her anguish but still the *kepala adat*, looked round for the young girl who was to have been Tia's replacement. But she too was in a state of collapse, and they couldn't wait for her to recover. The Maro must be completed before dawn.

He was still casting round desperately for a solution when a figure touched him on the arm. She was already wearing the palm-frond mask, and it took him a while to recognize her; but as soon as he did, he waved frantically to the musicians; the music started again; the people cleared the ground; and Ibu Suri began to dance.

It must have been more than sixty years since she had last taken a solo part, but she shed those years like water.

Ibu Suri danced and young Suri reappeared, flowing flawlessly into the form of Hainuwele. She spun and turned, she swayed and pivoted, easing power out of interstices in the earth and weaving it into a net to protect the people. It was impossible to believe that this was not tiny Frond of the Coco Palm herself, back in the willowy young flesh, returning to her moment of glory in the Maro.

On and on she flew, picking up all the threads of the dance and uniting them into a totally cohesive whole that mirrored the original mystery of creation. In her hands and at her feet the soul was renewed and born again, entering into life and reaffirming the mysterious as an essential ingredient of existence.

As she whirled into the final turns, dust was whipped into the air by a convoy of winds that blasted across the plain, heralds of a storm that felt the dawn and was prepared to wait no longer.

At the very instant that the Maro and the music ended, light from the rising sun touched the tip of Gunung Api and lightning flashed out of the dark cloud rolling round the hills at its feet.

A solid wall of rain came sweeping across the stubble in the rice fields, sending the people fleeing down the path back to the village.

And when it hit the place of the Nine Dance Grounds, only an old woman with long gray hair was there, shredding a palm-frond mask in her wrinkled hands, oblivious of the downpour that washed her tears away almost as fast as they fell.

FINAL STATE

AIR

Each of us carries, in addition to his assumed burdens, the weight of more than ten tons of air on his back. The only reason we are not squashed flat is that within our blood and body fluids we hold more air under pressure, pushing outwards.

The two forces are held in precarious equilibrium, and constant unconscious attention to detail in this matter gives us a special sensitivity to minute variations, both near and far. We are as much part of the ocean of air as every fish and djuru is of that lower denser ocean, the sea.

Sometimes it is difficult to bring such information through the filters of the brain to the attention of consciousness, but there is always help available.

Three days before the Maro began, something happened to the evening chorus of drongos, bulbuls, parrots, flycatchers, and cockatoos. It began with a few subtle changes in theme and tone, but these became progressively more elaborate and emphatic *until everyone agreed that the birds had changed their tune.*

Listen to them. They are always the first to know when there are changes in the air.

The Garden Gate

The storm raged for three days.

When it was over, the people looked around them and found that much had changed.

Tia had disappeared.

For days we searched the island, but there was no trace of her anywhere. Abu went round the entire coast in his prau, watching the water and the shore in case she had drowned, but when nothing turned up after three more days, he gave up and reconciled himself to her death.

The people talked a lot about the things she had done, and about things in which she had never been involved at all, and soon her life began to acquire an almost mythical quality. She became remote and indefinable, the kind of magic thing that never was, but is always happening.

The people all felt very close to her, or to their memory of her, and began to examine the growing myth for meaning. Tia's gentleness became an inspiration, a pattern and example for the children.

Tia's strength grew until it provided a new incentive for everyone.

All the talk made me miserable.

On the days after the Maro I had begun to suspect that Tia had set the whole thing up deliberately; that she had sought her own crucifixion, choosing the time and place so that in the end she would shatter of her own accord, allowing the fragments to find their proper place.

It looked to me in the end as though Marduk and all his generation had been merely tools in her design, perhaps even part of her own substance. Her flesh yielded willingly, and the agent, her apparent enemy, the hand that did the carving, was actually part of her will.

But when the sun came out again this seemed ridiculous. Then all I could remember was her frail form and the tears of desolation at the end. And I grew angry and impatient with the people and their mythmaking and wondered whether it had all been in vain.

Ibu Suri looked very old and tired, so I sought out Pak Moudhi in search of solace.

He was his usual philosophic self and tried very hard to explain to me that although life was stained with agony, this was necessary. That scars only concealed, and finally helped to reveal, an essential peace. He said that what we, who pass so swiftly, experience as songs of love or cries of pain are only overtones to a single note in a very much larger harmony.

He put it well; but I was, and still am, too young to come to terms with this all at once.

I could see that Marduk was a new man—very gentle; almost intuitive in his dealings with people. But for some reason this pushed me even deeper into despair.

I felt ill equipped to deal with the new situation and for the first time ill at ease on the island.

So when the Bugis returned a week later, I jumped at the chance to leave and travel with them to Sulawesi.

We sailed out through Pintu at dawn, just as the first fingers of the new monsoon began to feel their way up out of the south and east beyond the island.

The farewells were warm, and I carried away with me a parting gift that tided me well over the long sea voyage.

Just as I was about to wade out to the prau, Pak Moudhi took me to one side.

"Peace on your going, Tuan," he whispered. "And go with this. Last evening I walked on the sand of Tanah Utara and saw a strange thing. Ganti was there at the water's edge. And in the shallows, very near the shore, was a large *lumba-lumba*."

He paused to see what effect this had on me, and added, "They were very much together."

The baton, it seemed, had been picked up almost before it touched the ground.

Ganti was the four-year-old daughter of Bebas the charcoal burner.

And *lumba-lumba* is *Stenella longirostris,* commonly known as the spinning or dancing dolphin.

SOURCES

All those who recognize the need for reconciliation between man and nature owe a debt to Loren Eiseley, who was the first scientist in our time to take on the language of poetry in order to communicate basic but fragile biological truths. His graceful essays are at their most gently persuasive in:

The Immense Journey, Random House, New York, 1957.
The Invisible Pyramid, Charles Scribner's Sons, New York, 1970.

Amongst his heirs, I value most:

Annie Dillard in *Pilgrim at Tinker Creek*, Jonathan Cape, London, 1975; Harper's Magazine Press, New York 1974.

Lewis Thomas in *The Lives of a Cell*, Viking Press, New York, 1974.

The best introduction to Earthing and the notion of power points and places is:

John Michell's *The View over Atlantis*, Garnstone Press, London, 1972.

For humanity in the study of man, I recommend:

Edmund Carpenter in *Oh, What a Blow That Phantom Gave Me!*, Holt, Rinehart and Winston, New York, 1973.

And for balance in psychic research:

Lawrence Le Shan's *The Medium, The Mystic and The Physicist*, Viking Press, New York, 1974.

The concepts of the new physics are most intelligibly expressed in:

David Bohm's paper "Quantum Theory as an Indication of a New Order in Physics" in *Quantum Theory and Beyond*, edited by Ted Bastin, Cambridge University Press, 1971.

Bob Toben's discussion with Jack Sarfatti and Fred Wolf in *Space Time and Beyond*, E. P. Dutton and Co., New York, 1975.

The chapters by Evan Harris Walker, Harold Puthoff and Russell Targ in Edgar Mitchell's *Psychic Exploration*, G. P. Putnam's Sons, New York, 1974.

John A. Wheeler's *The Physicist's Conception of Nature*, Reidel Publications, Amsterdam, 1974.

The most lucid report of strange phenomena is the first-person account by:

Matthew Manning in *The Link*, Colin Smythe, Gerrards Cross, 1974.

The most courageous attempt to come to terms with these happenings is:

John Taylor's *Superminds*, Macmillan, London, 1975; Viking Press, New York, 1975.

And, for celebration of the presence and significance of whales and dolphins there is no more meaningful assembly than:

Joan McIntyre's *Mind in the Waters*, Charles Scribner's Sons, New York, 1974.

For further reading…

The Nature of Things
The Secret Life of Inanimate Objects
Lyall Watson
ISBN 0-89281-408-X • $12.95 pb

We have all experienced those strange moments when things seem to take on a life of their own. Valued possessions return to their owners, houses take on a welcome or unfriendly demeanor, lost items reappear in unlikely places, and computers misbehave. What exactly is going on? In this fascinating book, visionary biologist Lyall Watson asks some serious questions about such occurrences. Are we witnessing the development of a new life-form? Are we investing objects with a life force through the attention we give them? Watson explores the subtle forces of memory fields and suggests that matter has the capacity to absorb emotional "fingerprints," the mental fossils that channel echoes from the past. Through stories of sacred stones that sing, lost wedding rings that reappear, and statues of the Virgin Mary that weep, Watson demonstrates the complexity of inanimate life and offers possible proof of our sensitivity to its minute, natural patterns of energy.

"There is nothing worse than a closed mind. Lyall Watson has a first-rate scientific brain. His strength lies in his readiness to find and study strange phenomena without the fears that other scientists have." **Desmond Morris**
Author of *The Naked Ape*

The Dreams of Dragons

An Exploration and Celebration
of the Mysteries of Nature

Lyall Watson
ISBN 0-89281-372-5 • $9.95 pb

Prowling the edges of science with insight and sensitivity, Lyall Watson maintains that there is a truth to be found behind every seemingly impossible legend. Here, he takes us on a journey that winds through prehistoric burial sites on the beaches of South Africa, ancient iron mines in Swaziland, and present day villages in Indonesia and New Guinea inhabited by man-eating dragons and headhunters. In these and other extraordinary travels we encounter phenomena that defy traditional scientific explanation. The author's investigations bring to light the ordered patterns of "chance," the extrasensory perception of animals, the aquatic ancestry of the human species, and the electromagnetic resonance among all living things. Watson looks beyond the scientific "facts" and helps us—through his logical investigations of illogical events—to see the poetry and wonder of the natural world.

The Rebirth of Nature

The Greening of Science and God

Rupert Sheldrake

ISBN 0-89281-510-8 • $14.95 pb

Rupert Sheldrake, one of the world's foremost biologists, has revolutionized scientific thinking with his vision of a living, developing universe with its own inherent memory. In *The Rebirth of Nature* Sheldrake urges us to move beyond the centuries-old mechanistic view of nature, explaining why we can no longer regard the world as inanimate and purposeless. Through an astute critique of the dominant scientific paradigm, Sheldrake shows how recent developments in science itself have brought us to the threshold of a new synthesis in which traditional wisdom, intuitive experience, and scientific insight can be mutually enriching.

"A beautifully written, deeply felt, and sinuously argued challenge to many habits of thought." **Booklist**

"This frontal assault on conventional science embodies a radical rethinking of humanity's place in the scheme of things." **Publishers Weekly**

"A sterling reassessment of humankind's attitudes toward science and spirituality...Sheldrake has the scientific schooling to back up his eco-think." **Kirkus Reviews**

Ring of Fire

An Indonesian Odyssey

Lawrence Blair with Lorne Blair
ISBN 0-89281-430-6 • $24.95 pb • 272 pages, 8 1/2 x 11
More than 100 full color and black and white photographs

The true story behind the internationally award-winning PBS television series, *Ring of Fire* charts the Blair brothers' ten-year journey through the world's largest and least-known archipelago—the islands of Indonesia. Amid seemingly impenetrable rainforests, erupting volcanoes, and unimaginable natural beauty, the brothers captured on film and in words the customs, beliefs, and wisdom of the islands' inhabitants.

Their odyssey began with a 2500 mile voyage through the Spice Islands, guided by the notorious Bugi pirates. An entire decade of exploration followed, during which the authors lived among cannibals in West New Guinea and the sages and healers of Bali; encountered the man-eating dragons of Komodo and the elusive "dream wanderers" of Borneo; and learned legends of starship ancestors in the Celebes highlands. With extraordinary courage, humor, and passion for the unknown, they tell the story of one of the most captivating and intriguing journeys ever made, which will stand as an enduring record of a vanishing world.

"Incomparable adventure teeming with thrills, chills, mystery, and the bizarre."
Los Angeles Times

"Sets sails and sights for lands as unfamiliar and spectacular as anything dreamed up for a Steven Spielberg movie. Thoroughly fascinating nearly every harrowing step of the way." **Washington Post**

Rhythms of Vision

Changing Patterns of Myth and Consciousness

Lawrence Blair

ISBN 0-89281-320-2 • $12.95 pb

In this thought-provoking book, Blair maintains that throughout history, patterns of belief have shifted like cycles of tides in a vast rhythm, from eras where myth is a living reality to the times when reason reigns supreme. Today, the pendulum seems to be swinging again, as we begin to believe that science and technology may not have all the answers, and we seek new patterns of myth and consciousness that will incorporate both the feeling and rational aspects of our nature.

The author contends that we are poised on the threshold of a new age of thought—one that will reject assumptions based purely on tangible, measurable evidence. He maintains that the intuitions of myth, the ancient occult arts, and the mystical and prophetic rituals of religion compose a core of energy-rhythms that converge with scientific discoveries at the frontier of contemporary thought.

"This is a difficult book. And an important one…it expects us to question our most basic beliefs, those tidy interpretations of reality that we have all learned to make in common and to accept as exclusive fact." **Lyall Watson**

These and other Inner Traditions/Destiny Books titles are available at many fine bookstores or to order directly from the publisher, please send a check or money order payable to Inner Traditions for the total amount, plus $3.50 shipping and handling for the first book and $1.00 for each additional book to:

Inner Traditions, P.O. Box 388, Rochester, VT 05767
1-800-246-8648 • Be sure to request a free catalog
Visit our Web site: www.InnerTraditions.com